As deeply caring as she is wise, deep,
has written for all who are suffering and in pain. She has been there
herself, and she also knows the sure path to comfort, healing and faith.
A book to be read slowly and cherished—and shared with others who
are in pain.

Os Guinness
Author, *Unspeakable*

This book arises out of the conviction of the author that if Christian
faith is worth considering, it needs to be deep enough to cope with our
most rigorous human scrutiny and our most heart-rending questions.
Amy is not afraid to address the "why" questions, and that of suffering
and pain is the hardest of all for any of us. With a sympathetic heart
and a probing, honest mind, she helps the reader think through a
wide range of causes of our pain and distress, and introduces us to the
incomparable grace of the Good Shepherd, who himself suffered and
gave his life for the sheep. A book to be read and shared—especially in
this time of global pain."

Professor John C. Lennox
Emeritus Professor of Mathematics, University of Oxford

This is a brilliant and beautifully written introduction to the thorniest
issue of all time by one of the sharpest thinkers I know. Drawing on
ancient wisdom and contemporary thought, Amy Orr-Ewing brings
refreshing clarity, empathy and hope to the question that taunts and
haunts the human soul: *Where is God in all the suffering?* Everyone
should read this book.

Pete Greig
Author, *God on Mute: Engaging the Silence of Unanswered Prayer*

This remarkable book, written in a clear and engaging style, is a "must
read" for Christians and non-Christians, young and old. The author
is a gifted communicator and combines vivid first-hand experiences
with thorough, sound theological reflections and biblical commentar-
ies. No human life is devoid of suffering in one form or another; all
can benefit from what has been lived and recorded here.

The Most Rev Dr. B.A. Kwashi
Archbishop of Jos, Nigeria

Many assume that suffering in the world proves that God is simply not real, especially when we consider severe suffering. Amy Orr-Ewing, in her candid, open-hearted, intellectually rigorous and beautifully written book, shows that the very opposite is true. Amy tackles some of the very worst forms of suffering that we face, and shows that even in the deepest, darkest, most depraved recesses of our world, the case for a loving God still stands. Whether you have intellectual questions or are in deep pain, you will find *Where is God in all the Suffering?* extremely helpful. I highly recommend it.

Sharon Dirckx
OCCA The Oxford Centre for Christian Apologetics;
author, *Why? Looking at God, evil and personal suffering*

In an extraordinary combination of argument and empathy, Amy Orr-Ewing weaves together the Bible story of suffering and her own experience as a woman, a wife, a mother, an academic, a pastor and a friend. And this in turn enables her to ask the reader, "What is your story so far?" Such a timely book for these days of COVID-19.

Rico Tice
All Souls Church, London; Founder, Christianity Explored

Amy Orr-Ewing isn't afraid to face the tough questions in life, and in this brilliant book she takes on one of the toughest of all. The fact that she does so not only with a sharp intellect but with a compassionate heart makes this a very unique read. No one escapes suffering, and Amy's wonderfully wise words will be a helpful guide and a healing balm for so many.

Matt Redman
Christian Worship Leader; Singer-Songwriter; Author

The strongest argument against a loving God is the presence of human suffering. This truly helpful book brings to this daunting subject a profound realism, a warm sympathy and a deep Christian faith. Highly recommended!

J. John
Pastor; Author; Broadcaster

Where is God in all the Suffering?

AMY ORR-EWING

Where is God in all the Suffering?
© Amy Orr-Ewing, 2020

Published by:
The Good Book Company in partnership with
OCCA The Oxford Centre for Christian Apologetics and The Zacharias Institute

thegoodbook.com | www.thegoodbook.co.uk
thegoodbook.com.au | thegoodbook.co.nz | thegoodbook.co.in

Amy Orr-Ewing has asserted her right under the Copyright, Designs and Patents
Act 1988 to be identified as the author of this work.

A CIP catalogue record for this book is available from the British Library.

Unless indicated, all Scripture references are taken from the Holy Bible, New
International Version (NIV). Copyright © 2011 Biblica, Inc. Used by permission.

New Living Translation (NLT). Copyright © 2015 Tyndale House Foundation.
Used by permission.

ISBN: 9781784982768 | Printed in Turkey

Design by André Parker

Contents

Introduction: *A world in pain*   7

1. Asking "Why?"   13

2. Anger   27

3. Grief   39

4. Sickness   51

5. Mental Illness   65

6. Violence   83

7. Natural Disasters   95

8. Systemic Suffering   107

9. The Suffering Servant   117

Conclusion   127

Acknowledgements   133

For my boys, Zac, JJ and Benji Orr-Ewing.

With love always.

Introduction:
A world in pain

As I write this, my dear friend Brenda has just died. She was 36 and leaves a husband and three children, the youngest of whom is a five-month-old baby.

A few days ago I walked behind her casket into her funeral service, carrying her baby girl in my arms. I find myself asking: is there any hope in this seemingly hopeless situation? Is there any comfort for a daughter who will grow up not remembering her mother? Is there a loving God who could pour his love and comfort into our grieving hearts? Is God really there in all our pain and heartache over loss?

Right now I find myself working at home during a government lockdown, in isolation with my family. The death toll from COVID-19 climbs daily. We have all been shocked to discover how vulnerable and helpless we are against a microbial virus that has taken loved ones, closed borders, shops and restaurants, and halted the economy of half the planet. Where is God in the fear, suffering and grief of this global pandemic?

As you have picked up this book and started to read, I'm assuming that you want to think, to question and to consider what it means to be in pain and where God might be in the midst of that. But I want you to know at the very start that I don't want to attempt to "fix" you, or to "fix" how you experience pain. Rather, I hope my reflections here might be a helpful and comforting companion to you as you think about where God might be in this world filled with suffering.

Books on suffering written by academic types rarely connect with people who are actually suffering. I work in Oxford, and I have had the opportunity of studying and teaching throughout my adult working life. In the course of that time, I have found myself drawn to thinking about and reflecting on some of the toughest questions of life. Through all of that, I have come to realise that if Christian faith is worth considering, it needs to be deep enough to cope with our most rigorous human scrutiny *and* our most heart-rending questions.

JUST HAVE FAITH?

One of the worst things people in religious circles some-times seem to say to someone suffering is "Don't ask why", closely accompanied by "Don't think about it" or "Just have faith." These comments are just so unhelpful.

A questioning and thoughtful response to our human experience of suffering can be a really important part of coming to terms with terrible things that have happened to us. But I want to suggest that it can also be a crucial part of exploring the Christian faith. The Bible is full of people's questions to and about God in the context of human suf-fering. Questions like *Why would you let this happen?* and *Where are you, God?* So, if you are reading this book while you are going through an experience of personal suffering that is causing you to question and rethink everything, I'd like to thank you for letting me be a part of your journey. I hope that as you reflect on some of the thoughts offered in this book, you will find that Christian faith can be a warm home both for those who are intellectually curious and for anyone who finds themselves in a season of pain. Questions and doubts are not dangers to be avoided or suppressed but can be companions on a journey towards a relationship with God, and a genuine exploration of faith.

WHERE I AM COMING FROM

There are other things about me that you might like to know before we embark on this voyage together. Am I an ivory-tower academic coming at this question as a puzzle to be solved?

No…

My own personal experience has graphically coloured this question of suffering for me. Although I am a writer, a thinker and a teacher, I have spent 14 years of my life living in deprived neighbourhoods—in the inner city. I lived for seven years at a time in two of Britain's most disadvantaged and dangerous neighbourhoods. As a teenage girl I was physically attacked, but, perhaps more significantly, in my early thirties I lived under the specific threat of violent attack (rape and murder) for two years.

As a pastor I have also walked closely with loved ones who are suffering. When you hold a dying child in your arms in a hospice and weep with friends over the loss of their child, it is clear that well-meaning theories about purpose in suffering ring hollow. I once heard an academic at a conference sincerely offer the view that human suffering can be likened to a dog being taken to the vet for vaccinations. The dog can't see the purpose in the suffering, even though it is ultimately for its good. *Really?* I was completely floored by that illustration and actually quite angry. Listening to and crying with heroic survivors of sexual and domestic violence or the relatives of murder victims colours my approach to this question of discovering a God of love in our suffering world—as do my experiences of walking closely with people who experience the more day-to-day challenges of grinding poverty, debt, extortion, harassment and decay.

Personal experience inevitably shapes our thoughts about the question of suffering and evil, and we all need to be honest about that. For me this question is profoundly personal; it is not primarily abstract or theoretical. How do we make sense of the suffering in the world around us when it feels like *this*?

UP CLOSE AND PERSONAL

Even closer to home, as I write this, my husband and I are processing together the full extent of the abuse he experienced as a child. New discoveries about the horror of the things done to him have come to light in documents that came into our possession. It has taken us weeks to muster the emotional energy to read the pages of legal testimony and hospital reports. At times it has felt as if we are looking evil directly in the face. The person I share my life most closely with has been subjected to unimaginable trauma.

Wondering why a loving God might allow suffering, or, for that matter, where he is while we suffer, are not questions that any of us can dissect with sterilised instruments in a clean laboratory removed from outside influence or bias or personal pain. Because, even as we ask these questions, we live *here*—in this world—where brutal, senseless, tragic things happen to people we love. This book is intended to be a reflection from the perspective of Christian faith in the midst of this dark world on *why* there might be such suffering in this world *if* God is loving, and *how* God—if he exists at all—interacts with people who are in pain.

When my university friend died in a freak accident while travelling in South America a year after our graduation, a whole crowd of us in our 20s, just starting our first jobs, gathered at his funeral. I remember one of them saying, "Is pain the price we pay for love?" Grief was, and is, a strange and disconcerting experience. Grief involves fear, sadness, tears, a sense of shock and maybe even a disconnect from the loss. And then, as life goes on, the intense feelings subside only to suddenly and unexpectedly resurface. One moment life is bumbling along, and then suddenly, out of nowhere, a wave of sorrow and sadness hits, crashing over you, threatening to drown you, sucking the very life from your lungs. You realise that the person you have lost is not there and you will never see their face again.

THE PRICE OF LOVE

A Hebrew poet in Psalm 23 in the Bible powerfully describes this experience as "the valley of the shadow of death". This shadow is cast most profoundly over those who loved the person who has died most intimately, but it touches all who knew them. So, as my friend asked, *Is pain the price of love?*

At the funeral of the child of some dear friends, the service began with the thought that this precious newborn baby boy had never known a day without love. The pain and grief of those who loved him most was the cost of that love. He was loved.

For me, love is the starting place for untangling questions of pain and suffering, and especially the question "Where is *God* in all the suffering?" Love seems to be at the absolute core of why suffering feels like it does. Suffering feels so wrong to us because of our love for another person who is in distress. We instinctively rage against injustice because we feel that people deserve love and dignity. And when I suffer, the question I am struggling with at the deepest level is this: *Am I loved?* And if I am truly loved, *how could this be happening to me?*

When we ask these kinds of questions, we are making an assumption: that people have inherent and sacred value by virtue of being human; that *I* have value because I am human. But can we take for granted that love is a foundational concept from which to ask questions about suffering and God? As we try to wrap our heads around the human experience of suffering and the question of where God is in suffering—is love really that important? Aren't there other ways of looking at this question that are not grounded in a relational perspective and all that follows from the prospect of the existence of a loving God? Can we even meaningfully say that suffering is *wrong*, rather than simply unlucky?

It is these questions we explore first.

Asking "Why?"

"I see the world gradually being turned into a wilderness. I hear the ever-approaching thunder, which will destroy us too. I can feel the sufferings of millions and yet, if I look up into the heavens, I think that it will all come right, that this cruelty too will end, and that peace and tranquillity will return again."

ANNE FRANK

Whatever your beliefs about the world—why we are here, whether there is purpose to our existence, why there is so much pain in the world, whether there is a God, and what that God may or may not be like—at some point most of us are likely to find ourselves asking the question "why?" And this often happens during an experience of pain. The instinct to ask "why?" is deeply human.

When I was 29, I gave birth to twin boys. I've been asked the question "What's it like having twins?" so many times that you would think I would have a quick and pithy answer by now. But I always stop and take a deep breath because it is so hard to put into words—it's an incredibly intense experience. When twins are toddlers, it is so utterly exhausting that, although it is often wonderful, it can be completely overwhelming. Simple things like eating, getting dressed or going outside with the pushchair created untold chaos.

When my boys were starting to speak and to formulate their thoughts into words, they both went through a stage of asking "Why?" in stereo to every single thing that was said to them or asked of them. I once counted 98 different occurrences of the "why" question from them in a single morning. I made a note of it in my diary. The phase went on for weeks. Somehow I held on to my sanity and lived to tell the tale. But "why" questions stand out to me now as profoundly human. As human beings it seems we are wired to ask "why?"

As we reflect together on the question of suffering, and consider why it happens, why it hurts so much and where God might be in it all, there are many different potential starting points. Human beings have wondered, written and thought about pain and suffering since time immemorial. But not every framework of thought begins with love. Should we take love for granted as a starting place in exploring pain, grief and suffering? Why would love matter so much?

IS IT KARMA?

You may be aware that Eastern philosophy views human suffering through the dual lenses of karma and reincarnation. When something painful happens, karma tells me that there is a moral law of cause and effect guiding the circumstances of our lives. If I get a disease or have an accident, the law of karma means I am getting what I deserve. The fact that the thing I have done that makes me deserve pain may not immediately be obvious to me is complicated by the idea of reincarnation. In this view, the universe recycles us over multiple lifetimes, so, it is believed, we may be experiencing the effects of karma for something done in a previous life.

I had a neighbour for a couple of years in Oxford who believed that she had been a member of the French resistance in a previous life. She felt that her failure to pass on a particular message in time during the war was the cause of her back pain in this life. Karma was running its course. Karma does not love. Suffering is inflicted by a faceless system of law, leaving us with what it determines we deserve.

Buddhism encourages its followers to seek detachment as a way of processing suffering. The Buddha left his wife and home on the night that his first child was born. He left his palace in order to seek enlightenment, and that meant moving away from emotional bonds to become detached from them and this world. Buddhist enlightenment is essentially following the Buddha's example in choosing disconnection from everything.

Human suffering, he taught, comes from desire. Wanting, desiring something or someone is at the root of suffering, so the Buddhist answer is to expunge all desire for anything or anyone: to cease wanting things and to reach a state of enlightenment—which is a kind of nothingness. Is pain the cost of love? This way of looking at the world would answer "yes"; and so, to avoid pain, the answer offered is to get rid of all attachment—even love. Where is God in this system of thinking? Nowhere and everywhere. God is not a personal being but rather a state of realisation that all is one and one is all.

IS IT FATE?

Islam gives us a different perspective. It has a monotheistic view of the world—there is one God—but it is a fatalistic religion teaching that a transcendent God is absolutely and directly in control of every aspect of the universe. As a consequence, human beings do not have real choice. There is only one will in the universe, and that is Allah's will. That is why the word *inshallah,* meaning *"if-God-wills-it"* is so significant for Muslims.

A few years ago a friend described to me his experience of training a group of Iraqi soldiers for service in their own armed forces. He was required to take them through a survival exercise, and so they took over a disused swimming pool and filled it with water. The British officer explained that each person, fully clothed and carrying their heavy pack, would be pushed into the deep end of the pool. The goal was to swim to the surface, tread water for a certain amount of time and then to climb out.

The first two recruits were selected and thrown fully clothed into the deep end. One struggled to the surface and then clambered out of the pool, but the other sank like a stone. The instructors quickly realised there was a problem and one dived in, dragged the man to the surface and pumped his chest. The man coughed up water and gasped for air. "Why didn't you swim?" they shouted at him. He shrugged and replied, "If it be God's will that I live, I would live; if it be his will that I die, I would have died. Clearly it was God's will that I lived." *Inshallah.* I embrace my fate because it is the will of God.

This illustrates the extent to which a mindset of God's will being all that matters can influence our way of seeing the world and acting in it. And logically since both good and evil exist, they must both be God's will.[1] In other words, from this widespread perspective, when we are in pain we can conclude that everything that is happening to us is directly God's will. God is the author of it all and so we may as well just accept it. Love doesn't really come into it. And neither does asking "why?"

IS IT MEANINGLESS?

A different point of view is offered by what we might call naturalism. Naturalism is the system derived from the belief that everything in life has a purely natural or physical explanation. In answer to the question "Where is God in all the suffering?" naturalism would say, "*Nowhere*—because God doesn't exist." Naturalism tells us that there is no spiritual or religious dimension to life and there is no God who created the natural world. Human beings are their own highest authority and are well able to determine their own destiny and their own morality. Within this way of looking at the world, any experience of pain is essentially random; it is a consequence of living in the physical world and nothing more. And since the physical biochemical world is all that exists, any sense of connection to another person and love for them is viewed in primarily physiological terms. The pain I may experience as a result of the loss of someone I am connected to does not have any deeper metaphysical or spiritual dimensions. Suffering, like everything else, is merely physical, material and natural.

---

1   Muhammad was asked about this and his reply is recorded in the Hadith: "Abu Bakr asserts that Allah decrees good, but does not decree evil, but Umar says that he decrees both alike. Muhammad replied to this 'the decree necessarily determines all that is good and all that is sweet and all that is bitter, and that is my decision between you ... O Abu Bakr if Allah had not willed that there be disobedience he would not have created the Devil'."
Quoted in Arthur Jeffrey, *Islam: Muhammad and His Religion*, p 150.

When it comes to pain or suffering that has a more obvious and directly moral dimension, this is particularly significant. For example, if a woman is sexually assaulted, naturalism has not rooted morality objectively in God ("sexual assault is wrong in absolute terms and God is the ultimate judge of this"). Instead, it has rooted morality subjectively either in personal preference ("I do not want this to happen to me or those I love therefore it is wrong") or in societal taboo ("As a society we can see this is damaging and so we need to create laws to make sure it doesn't happen"). As the author and champion of atheistic naturalism Richard Dawkins said in a radio interview, "We supply our own basis for ethics."

Many people think that suffering is a problem for those who believe in God. But the problem of suffering does not disappear when we get rid of God. The great atheist French philosopher and writer Jean-Paul Sartre observed that a culture that had stopped believing in God was left with real questions about pain and suffering as well as good and evil. He put it like this:

> ... for there disappears with Him [God] all possibility of finding values in an intelligible heaven. There can no longer be any good a priori, since there is no infinite and perfect consciousness to think it ... Nor, on the other hand, if God does not exist, are we provided with any values or commands that could legitimise our behaviour. Thus, we have neither behind us, nor before us in a luminous realm of values, any means of justification or excuse.[2]

---

2   Jean-Paul Sartre, *Existentialism Is a Humanism* (Yale University Press, 2007), p 28, www.marxists.org/reference/archive/sartre/works/exist/sartre.htm (accessed 5th April 2020).

More recently, however, atheists have argued alongside believers in God that a personal or contractual basis for morality is not enough. Believers in God have often pointed out that when you look at the suffering world, you should ask yourself whether personal preferences or societal contracts are enough to underpin morality? After all, didn't Islamic State (also known as ISIL or Daesh) sincerely believe in what they were doing in Syria and Iraq? Who are we to say that their personal preferences or the morality of their society organised around a Caliphate is wrong? Don't racists believe they are morally right in their delusions of superiority, and haven't racist societies even legalised such notions— who are we to say they are wrong? In some cultures, such things may be acceptable and legal; some regimes have even made mass murder legal. This was the case as recently as the twentieth century in Europe, yet we instinctively know that this must be wrong. Philosophers have pointed out that this moral conclusion only makes sense if there is an ultimate reference point for morality—a source of morality transcending us and our societies—and that this is a good reason to believe in God.

But now atheists such as Erik Wielenberg argue that we don't actually need God for this ultimate morality; we can just point to some "brute moral facts" as existing above preference or societal legislation, and we don't need God as their source for them to be absolute. There are a number of issues around this position. While believers in God might only need to propose the brute fact of God being the source and definition of what is truly "good", with morality flowing from that, atheists would need to posit multiple brute moral facts, making it a weaker position on a purely philosophical level. And perhaps more significantly, atheism would need to account for our human ability to know or discern such moral facts. On what basis could we trust the cognitive ability of our own human reason if we arrived here in the universe by an unguided process of random chance? How could the brute moral facts suggested by some be reliably recognised and known by blobs of atoms who came about by chance? Realistically, it still seems to be the case that objective morality is not clearly established or recognisable without the existence of an ultimate moral authority—God. And so our sense that wrongs which cause suffering are outrageous and wrong points to God existing as the judge of such things, and as the creator who has made human beings with the capacity to reason, choose and love.

THE HUMAN EXPERIENCE OF SUFFERING

But, perhaps a deeper and more personal question for advocates of naturalism to consider in all of this is our anguish as human beings in response to pain. If human life is not essentially sacred, but merely an accident of chance biology and chemistry, does our outrage and anguish in the face of suffering really make sense? Why would human beings really have any intrinsic worth and such a deep conscious and emotive response to pain and suffering without God, existing? Professor Peter Singer argues that in the absence of God human beings have no more value or moral intuition than any other animal:

> *Whatever the future holds it is likely to prove impossible to restore in full the sanctity of life view ... We can no longer base our ethics on the idea that human beings are a special form of creation made in the image of God and singled out from all other animals ... our better understanding of our own nature has bridged the*

> *gulf that was once thought to lie between ourselves and*
> *other species; so why should we believe that the mere*
> *fact that a being is a member of the species Homo Sa-*
> *piens endows its life with some unique almost infinite*
> *value?* [3]

Does human life have value? Does it really matter if thousands die in a global pandemic, without access to a ventilator and alone in order to protect loved ones from catching the virus? Can we hear of the deaths of young people in a classroom on the other side of the world, gunned down by an unstable classmate, and simply shrug our shoulders? When we watch a documentary about wildlife in Africa and observe a lioness catching a warthog, do we have similar reactions to when we watch a documentary about a serial killer murdering women? I think that human life *does* have essential value, and that our reactions to the sufferings of human beings—even those we don't know—points to this.

So we are left with a question: if it is the case that there is no God who gives human life value and a meaning and significance beyond our physical existence, then why do we as human beings care about massacres, hunger, injustice or the sufferings of other humans? Why does this darkness hurt so much? Why does suffering really matter? From where do we get our sense of essential worth and dignity? Our outrage in reaction to suffering—including the suffering of people we don't know—and our human experience of pain itself all confirm the common human intuition that there is more to life than some might say. Where is God in all the suffering? Perhaps it is worth exploring the possibility that our human

---

3   Peter Singer, "Sanctity of Life or Quality of Life?" http://digitalcollections.library. cmu.edu/awweb/awarchive?type=file&item=594077 (accessed 5th April 2020).

outrage at suffering points us beyond ourselves and prompts us to seek meaning and transcendence.

Amid the potential starting places for considering suffering—naturalism, Buddhism or Islam—there is another alternative, and it is this perspective that I hope we can spend some time exploring together in this book—it is the Judeo-Christian, and specifically Christian perspective. This point of view sets forth the premises that God really does exist; that God is a personal being; that God is essentially loving; and that God has made human beings in his image with a capacity to reason, choose and love. It could follow from this that suffering hurts us as human beings in such a profound and shocking way because human beings really do matter. We are divine-image-bearers, and so our lives and wellbeing are sacred. This would mean that pain and suffering will hurt us at more than a physical level. If God is real and God is loving, pain will be the cost of love. Real love is simply not possible without freedom of choice—compelled love is never love. The possibility of love entails the possibility of pain.

THE IMAGE OF GOD

In Genesis, the first book of the Bible, the author talks about human beings created in the image of God.

> *So God created mankind in his own image,*
> *in the image of God he created them;*
> *male and female he created them.* GENESIS 1 v 27

Christian faith claims that there is a "God-likeness" about us as human beings—that our lives are essentially valuable because we bear the divine image. Whether we believe in God or not, whoever we are, we are creatures of dignity. If that is true, the essential part of you that makes you *you* has a transcendent source. Your value is not imagined or invented—it is real, and its grounding is God's image in you.

The Bible's response to the question of *why* God allows suffering builds on this essential claim: that *every* human life bears God's image. The obvious question is this: if human beings have such worth and dignity then *why are we subjected to such sorrow, pain and suffering?* How could God be good in allowing it? Doesn't the pain in the world call into question not only God's goodness but his very existence?

The Bible talks in Genesis of a good God creating a good world. The first creation account rings with the repeated phrase "*And God saw that it was good*". Then God located the people he made in a specific context (a garden) where they had the ability to choose.

> *The LORD God took the man and put him in the Garden of Eden to work it and take care of it. And the LORD God commanded the man, "You are free to eat from any tree in the garden; but you must not eat from the tree of the knowledge of good and evil, for when you eat from it you will certainly die."*
>
> GENESIS 2 v 15-17

Since God made humans to have the capacity to love, they also had to have the opportunity to choose. For love to exist, freedom must exist. The dark side to human existence, which we see all around us in the injustice, selfishness and suffering of the world, must have an explanation—*why* is it there? What does the Christian faith say about that? The Bible locates an explanation for pain, evil and suffering in the context of people having the ability to love and so the ability to make choices.

As a teenager growing up in Birmingham I became friends with a girl whose parents were trying to force her into a marriage with someone she did not know. She was just 15, and she was afraid. She had reason to be afraid because a relative of hers had been in the same position a year earlier. She had tried to run away but had been knocked down by a car in the street dragged home and forcibly taken out of the country to marry. No one had seen her or heard from her again. My teenage friend knew she didn't want that—she wanted to love and be loved. She felt that being forced into a legal partnership by her parents with someone she did not know and then raped on a regular basis was the antithesis of love. She believed that the love she was capable of giving and receiving could not be compelled by another. Friends helped her get to a safe house.

For true love to be possible, it must be freely offered and received. We all know this to be the case.

In Genesis, after the description of humans being created in the image of God, there is a story about two people called Adam and Eve. They are living in a beautiful garden called Eden. It is a place of fruitfulness, happiness and relational harmony. Everything that has been made has been pronounced "good". There is a loving, harmonious relationship between the humans themselves, between humanity and the world, and between humanity and God—so much so that Adam and Eve are described as walking and talking with God in the garden in the cool of the day. The story tells us that all of the fruit on all of the many trees is available for the man and woman to eat except for one particular tree. There is beauty, there is harmony and there is intimacy as the creator of Eden and of the entire world walks with the man and the woman in that garden.

But the existence of that one tree which they have been warned not to eat from means that they have a real choice to make. In the context of a loving and harmonious relationship, a boundary has been set, and so they have the genuine capacity to choose. They could choose not to eat from this one of the many trees and so maintain the harmony of the relationship, or they can choose to ignore the boundary and do as they please. The existence of that choice demonstrates that they are not robots programmed and controlled by the creator; they have the independent decision-making capacity that makes meaningful and loving relationship possible. Both Adam and Eve exercise their right to choose, and eat the forbidden fruit.

This story, right at the beginning of the Bible, tells us that God, who is love, made a world in which love is possible and that this entails there being a world in which there is the possibility of choice. The idea put forward is that as human beings we have used our choices to harm as well as to love. That is why there is injustice, darkness, pain and suffering in this world. Genesis describes the impact of the choices we have made on ourselves, on other people and upon the very environment of the earth. The first humans chose not to love God but instead to try to *be* God—to be the final authority over what is right and what is wrong. As the story of the Bible unfolds, there is a sense of progression from Adam and Eve with their original decisions to the wider impact and consequences of multiple moments of selfishness spreading rapidly until the effects are felt by everyone—including those not directly or personally responsible for a particular poor decision. In other words, moral choices impact not only ourselves, but also others and the very fabric of the universe.

The Christian faith understands darkness and suffering as having come into the world as a direct result of our human exercise of moral choice. And so suffering is real; it hurts. And it *really* hurts because we are more than our biochemistry; we are not here by accident. Human life has a transcendent source, we are bearers of the image of God, and in some deep way we sense this in ourselves and others, even those we will never know intimately—even if we don't believe in God. Christian faith understands life to be precious at an ultimate level, and that means that it will matter at the deepest level when we or others are in pain. This might help us understand *why* the human experience of pain is so acute.

As we will see in the following chapters, love, relationship and freedom are not only intrinsically connected in the Christian story; they frame the universal human experience of pain. But in the Christian story there is more to be discovered because we are introduced to a God who is *with* us in pain, a suffering God, a God who is *for* us in pain. In the midst of our experiences of suffering, ill health, grief, anger and even violence, we find ourselves questioning: where is God? How could he allow such things to happen?

As we explore such experiences and questions we will consider whether it is really possible to encounter a God who is prepared to take sin, pain and evil upon himself and make a way for us to be forgiven and restored, and whether there might be a God who can deliver on his promise to wipe away the tears from our eyes if we will trust him.

Anger

*"Tell me about your despair, yours,
and I will tell you mine."*
MARY OLIVER

Those who work with people who are grieving note that there seem to be five common phases in an experience of grief. The stages are denial, anger, bargaining, depression and acceptance.[4]

Anger. For many of us an experience of pain brings out indignation and anger in us.

It was 14th June 2017 when a fire broke out in a 24-storey apartment block in west London called Grenfell Tower. Despite the valiant efforts of the London Fire Brigade, the fire engulfed the upper storeys of the building. It later became clear that the cladding that had been installed on the exterior of the tower to update its look on the London skyline, rather than being fireproof, was actually highly flammable. So when an old fridge caught fire due to an electrical fault in one of the apartments, the cladding acted as a funnel

---

4   Elisabeth Kubler-Ross and David Kessler, *On Grief and Grieving* (Simon and
     Schuster, 2014).

helping the fire to ravage the building, killing 72 people. Residents of the tower, which was predominantly social housing, had complained to the authorities about fire safety, and this added to a sense of public outrage even as the tower burned and then smouldered on the city's skyline for days. The chaotic days immediately after the fire involved searches for individuals, particularly children, as authorities sought to confirm who had been in each of the apartments that night and who had perished in the fire. The extreme heat of the fire and the subsequent lack of human remains made the task of identifying who had died even more difficult. Every street was quickly plastered with missing-persons posters. The faces of missing children and adults stared out from every lamp post and wall.

The local churches were at the forefront of the efforts to feed, clothe and comfort the displaced residents and one particular church—Latymer Community Church—started a prayer wall a few metres from the smoking remains of the tower. The whitewashed wall had prayers written all over it, and it became the focal point of the community's grief. Candles were lit and flowers left by it. Images of the wall were beamed around the world in daily news reports.

COMMUNAL GRIEF

The fire started on a Wednesday, and by Saturday many of the first responders and pastors had not slept. My husband, Frog, had been there helping out, and the church leaders on the ground invited us to come and help run an outdoor service for the community on the first Sunday after the fire. Over 1,000 people from the area gathered that Sunday morning in the street and under the railway arches. Some were weeping, and many just stood in stunned silence. A woman and her daughter who had been best friends with a mother and daughter who had both died in the fire collapsed crying and screaming into my arms. The woman told me of their loss, and as she spoke she let out a kind of moan and was physically shaking at the thought of them being burned up in the fire.

The feeling on the street that day was a combination of intense sorrow and rumbling anger. Anger that this could happen in London—one of the most affluent cities in the world. Anger that the authorities did not even seem to be on top of how many people had lost their lives. Anger at the decision to use cheap cladding on the building because it was for social housing. Anger that the cladding had turned out not to be fire resistant but was actually a fire accelerant. And all of that anger had a *rightness* about it. 72 people, including 18 children, had died a terrifying and excruciating death. In the service, my husband read a small passage from the Bible before sharing some thoughts in an address. The text included these words:

> *He heals the brokenhearted*
> *and binds up their wounds.*   PSALM 147 v 3

There was rapt silence as people huddled together trying to take in what had happened and perhaps wondering if there was really such a God. And then the passage goes on:

> *The LORD sustains the humble*
> *but casts the wicked to the ground.*   PSALM 147 v 6

The crowd spontaneously erupted into clapping and shouting. The instinctual grief and anger of a community found an outlet in celebrating the words of a Hebrew poet from around 2,500 years ago. *The wicked will be cast to the ground.*

The idea that the perpetrators responsible for what had happened might be thrown to the ground felt pretty appealing to us as we stood dazed in the street on a grey and cloudy day with the acrid smell of smoke still hanging in the air. It felt as if rage was rippling very close to the surface of the crowd.

At this point the first responders and London Fire Brigade told us that they needed to drive their engines out of the area and, since the gathering had taken over the road, this meant driving right through the middle of the service. For three exhausting and relentless days and nights, they had struggled to put the fire out, and the entire crowd stood and applauded them. News outlets carried the images around the world as the mourning community stood and clapped and cheered them through the centre of the crowd. These heroic firemen and women wept in their engines. Tears were pouring down many faces.

I wrote to a friend a couple of days afterwards:

> *It's all completely overwhelming, traumatic and yet strangely grace-filled—a distressed relative of a victim of the fire was on the Westway (the road overpass) above our heads threatening to jump into the crowd and end his life and, as Frog spoke, the police came and he calmed down. Through the singing of nine verses of "Amazing Grace" his life was saved.*

WHERE DOES OUR ANGER COME FROM?

When horrendous things happen to us or to those we love, when we experience loss and disappointment, it is a common and truly human reaction to feel anger. On one level this is completely right and appropriate. Should we not feel anger that precious people were burned alive in a block of flats in west London? And if it is true that all human life bears the image of God, then anger in the context of pain is not only to be expected; it is warranted.

Sometimes well-meaning religious people are afraid of this kind of anger and seek to short-circuit the process—as if anger necessarily leads us away from God. But the Bible actually gives voice to people in the midst of suffering and gives them the freedom to express frustration, grief, anger and disappointment including railing against God directly. God wants to relate to us and deal with us as we really are. It is as if the Scriptures are telling us that God is ok with us doubting him, being angry with him and expressing our hurt to him when we are in pain. Speaking honestly to God in our anger and pain is a far better way forward than to stand at a distance shaking our fists at God, or to think we can only speak to him when we are feeling calm and positive. Anger as a legitimate, even positive way of processing pain is consistent with the enormous value placed on a human life by God.

Outrage in the face of injustice, death, disease or violence makes sense to us as human beings because we instinctively sense that this is not the way things are meant to be. But is that impulse really rational? Does outrage at evil or pain actually make sense of our own wider beliefs about the world and about God?

What is the foundation of human outrage at evil and suffering if life does not have a transcendent source and we are nothing more than a collection of atoms that has learned how to think?

After Charles Darwin first published his book *On the Origin of Species*, a British economist Herbert Spencer, coined the phrase "survival of the fittest" to encapsulate Darwin's idea of natural selection. Spencer was comparing Darwin's theory to his own economic principles. The central idea was that those life forms best suited to their environment would survive and eventually less suitable attributes would be bred out of the population. When combined with a materialist outlook (that is, there is no God behind the universe and all that exists is physical matter), human beings are to be viewed as the product of chance, striving for our own survival and advancement. The inevitable conclusion of this viewpoint is that individuals must put themselves first in every decision; after all, what else is there other than me and mine?

Ayn Rand, the atheist thinker, socialite and author, died in 1983, but still hundreds of thousands of her books sell each year. She thought that an atheist simply *had* to be an egoist. She wrote:

> *Every honest man lives for himself. Every man worth calling a man lives for himself. The one who doesn't— doesn't live at all.*[5]

The great German atheist philosopher Friedrich Nietzsche said something similar:

> *I submit that egoism belongs to the essence of a noble soul ... other beings must naturally be in subjection, and have to sacrifice themselves.*[6]

In other words, atheism tells me that I will always put myself first, and other people I come across may well need to be sacrificed due to my priorities. This way of looking at

---

5   Ayn Rand, *We are the Living* (MacMillan, 1936), p 501.
6   Friedrich Nietzsche, *Beyond Good and Evil: Prelude to a Philosophy of the Future* (Penguin, 1990), p 72.

the world might justify my outrage when I suffer personally or when my blood relatives are harmed—but it does not appear to be able to account for our widespread anger about pain including that experienced by people who are not genetically connected to us or necessary for our survival.

A RADICAL ALTERNATIVE

Christianity began in a world that was dominated by self-centred egoism, and as it grew, it started to challenge this approach to life. Jesus was born into an occupied nation under the harsh and merciless system of the Roman Empire, where rulers ruled with a rod of iron. But Christianity ended up conquering that empire with a more powerful weapon—kindness. The early Christians had an experience of a God who loved them and had shown them mercy, and part of the deal in following Jesus was that those who had been forgiven by him must forgive others. They would not ignore cruelty including that which affected people they didn't know; instead they countered it by caring for the weak and the outcast, the widows and the orphans. They reached out to those in pain and regarded all people as equal. It was an utterly distinctive and countercultural lifestyle.

We are so familiar with churches and the symbolism of Christianity that we may not really know how it all started and how radical it was. In a discussion hosted by *The New Statesman*, the former Archbishop of Canterbury Rowan Williams spoke to philosopher and leading British atheist John Gray, who acknowledged that the Christian faith is the origin of the modern Western liberal value of not being cruel or tolerating cruelty towards others. Gray commented:

> *The distinctive contribution of Christianity ... is*
> *that if you think back to the ancient Roman world,*

> *then one feature that came in with Christianity was*
> *the idea that human beings, reflecting the nature of a*
> *Christian god, had some responsibility for not being*
> *cruel or not even tolerating cruelty.*[7]

A refusal to tolerate cruelty to others was a distinctive of the Christian faith in the ancient world.

Of course atheists and agnostics, as well as Christians, will experience anger and outrage in the face of the suffering of others. But my question is: what can account for that anger? If human beings are created in the image of God, as Christians believe, it would apply whether an individual happens to believe it or not. If life is in some way sacred, we will have different ways of seeing this and knowing it to be true. At the foot of the smoking ruin of Grenfell Tower, I experienced that truth in the eyes and actions of people I have never met, including many who would not call themselves religious. Together in the smoke, debris and anguish, we knew the lives of those who had perished were undeniably precious. The loss of those lives made us not only angry and distressed, but also filled us with compassion. I think that is best explained by the Christian faith and its commitment to the idea that all human life is precious because human beings are created in the image of God. Where is God in all the suffering? He is the one who grounds the sacredness of our loves and lives, so that when life is destroyed or a person we love is blighted, our instinctive outpouring of anger at these things points directly to him.

In Western liberal democracies, religion has a reputation for being bland, beige and insipid. There is this view that a person of faith should never feel angry, and that churchgoing

---

7   "Matters of life and death: Rowan Williams and John Gray in conversation",
     New Statesman, 28th November 2018.

is for lacklustre thinkers or feeble feelers. But as I read the Bible, I discover something quite different from formulaic organised religion droning on about doing good. There are whole books of the Bible devoted to crying out for social justice for the oppressed. There are songs and poems and stories that express both human pain and loss, and the anger and outrage of God at human injustice and suffering. Christian faith does not shut down our rage at the violence or injustice of this world—*it explains it.* That kind of anger has a place in the Christian story—our heartfelt cries for justice and judgment echo the heart of the Christian story itself.

If religious people seem like compliant do-gooders to you—out of touch with and a bit remote from the real world—it may come as a surprise to discover that the Bible gives powerful voice to human responses to pain that express deep questions and confusion that terrible things are happening. The psalmist asks:

> *My God, my God, why have you forsaken me?*
> *Why are you so far from saving me,*
> *so far from my cries of anguish?*
> *My God, I cry out by day, but you do not answer,*
> *by night, but I find no rest.*   PSALM 22 V 1-2

And Jesus himself quoted these verses during his crucifixion. In another psalm the poet honestly and bluntly expresses his questions as to why God is permitting the pain and suffering he's experiencing:

> *I say to God my Rock,*
> *"Why have you forgotten me?*
> *Why must I go about mourning,*
> *oppressed by the enemy?"*

My bones suffer mortal agony
  as my foes taunt me,
saying to me all day long,
  "Where is your God?"   PSALM 42 v 9-10

The book of Job tells the story of a man who later in life was commended as a "righteous man", but who experiences terrible suffering. At one point he says:

Does it please you [God] to oppress me,
to spurn the work of your hands,
while you smile on the plans of the wicked?"

JOB 10 v 3

The prophet Habakkuk asks how long he is expected to continue shouting out to God that there is violence, pain and injustice while God appears to do nothing about it:

How long, LORD, must I call for help, but you do not
listen? Or cry out to you, "Violence!" but you do not
save?   HABAKKUK 1 v 2

Our human outrage when we see suffering or experience pain points to the fact that deep down we sense that things are not as they should be. We sense that the world ought to be a good place and that pain is spoiling it as people suffer all sorts of horrors around us. But why should we feel outrage if this material world of biology, physics and chemistry is all there is? Why should we feel disgust and fury at the unjust exploitation of children living on remote continents if human beings are merely the product of a random process of chance followed by the brutal outcome of a contest for the survival of the fittest? Why should our own pain or the pain of others matter?

However, anger in reaction to evil or pain *does* have a place in the Christian story—a place that gives voice and explanation to what we feel deep down. Our cries for justice and even for judgment carry with them the echoes of the Christian story. If we were made for love—if life has a transcendent source, if God's good image marks every human being, and if we have marred this world and each other with our choices—it is no surprise that we feel anger and even outrage when we experience evil. This is not how things are meant to be.

It is not uncommon when we face evil, pain and suffering to ask in anguish, "How much longer do I have to go through this?" But if the world is cold and meaningless, and we are nothing more than the physical arrangements of atoms, all of that sound and fury—all of our questions —mean nothing. But as we have seen, these same questions and frustrations articulated by people in pain are also found in the Bible. We are not alone if we express our anger and frustration to God—"How much longer are you going to let this go on?", "Why are you so distant?", "Why aren't you answering or helping?" In the Bible we are not left with a cold silence. An answer comes back that in the end makes real sense of our experience—affirming the validity of our outrage towards evil and promising that we need not be left floundering or alone in pain.

It is into the question of pain and connection that we turn in the next chapter as we consider the significance of grief and loss in our human experience of suffering, and ask "Where is God in all the suffering?" as we walk through grief.

Grief

"But for pain words are lacking."
VIRGINIA WOOLF

For most people a ride on Space Mountain at Disney World in Florida is a highlight of the trip. But as I inched my way forward to the front of the queue, I could feel the terror rising to the back of my throat.

Why did I let myself get talked into this?

As someone who suffers from motion sickness when driving a car on a straight road, I have never been one to seek thrills at amusement parks. But when I turned 40 some dear American friends very generously hosted our family for a few days at Disney. I was persuaded by the whole group to get into the queue for this roller coaster before I knew that most of the ride would happen in the dark. As the car climbed away from the light I knew I had made a mistake, but it was too late to back out—all I could do was close my eyes and hang on for dear life. When we got off the ride, everyone asked excitedly how I found it, and the politest and most British answer I could muster was "I coped!"

The experience of being hurled around with very sudden twists, turns and backwards loops that I couldn't see coming was utterly terrifying. But I think it is a pretty good analogy for grief. Grief can feel a bit like being a reluctant passenger on an accelerating roller coaster in pitch darkness: being thrown up and down, forwards and backwards, to the left and right, with no sense of what is coming next.

We have already heard that the Bible speaks of a loving God creating a world within which love is possible, since human beings have been made in his image, but in this chapter I would like us to consider how it also prepares us for the cost of that love—grief. The pain of loss is a very particular suffering reserved for anyone that has loved another person who has then died. In the human experience of grief, it becomes abundantly clear to us that love is not reducible to a biochemical firing of neurons or to raw animal survival instinct. But grief is so much more than that.

The Bible's account of human beings as god-like creatures given to each other as companions, lovers, friends and family, with the capacity to make deep and sacred attachments of love to each other, reflects the real lived experience of love between people in friendship, parenthood and marriage, and with our siblings. The English novelist and poet Dinah Craik wrote about the power and depth of human connection and friendship in the 1800s, and she describes it beautifully:

> But oh! the blessing it is to have a friend to whom one can speak fearlessly on any subject; with whom one's deepest as well as one's most foolish thoughts come out simply and safely. Oh, the comfort—the inexpressible comfort of feeling safe with a person—having neither to weigh thoughts nor measure words, but pouring them all right out, just as they are, chaff and grain together;

> *certain that a faithful hand will take and sift them,*
> *keep what is worth keeping, and then with the breath of*
> *kindness blow the rest away.*[8]

The joy of deep, unconditional friendship is so simple and yet utterly significant in life—it seems to be a uniquely human gift. Our friendships enrich life, connect us with the past and present, and, for many people, make life worth living. And so when death comes we experience it as more than the decay of physical tissue and basic matter—we experience it as loss. Yes, the loss of physical touch, but more devastatingly, the loss of emotional and sacred connection. Human suffering of this kind is a consequence of love.

UNEXPECTED GRIEF

I can still remember the exact street we were walking down in Florence, Italy, when the fateful phone call came through. We were on holiday as a family in Tuscany in the north of Italy, and we were spending a day in Florence, walking from the beautiful Duomo Cathedral to a monastery which has some stunning fourteenth-century frescos painted by the monk Fra Angelico. These are some of the most powerful paintings that I have ever seen, and I was excited that we were going to see them together as a family. Frog answered the phone as we continued to walk—it was his father's doctor. The news was bad. We needed to fly home immediately if we were to have any hope of seeing him alive and sentient.

We had been caring for my father-in-law through a bout of illness, but this was a completely shocking development. The next morning we were on a plane, and that afternoon we were at his side as a family. That was to be the last day my

8   Dinah Craik, *A Life for a Life* (Collins' Clear Type Press, 1900), p 63.

children ever saw their grandfather, and it is when they had the opportunity to say goodbye to him. The English summer was fading and so were the colours in the familiar garden. We ate outside together, surrounded by the smell of the lavender bushes, trying not to notice the gauntness of his body.

The following days were distressing and yet incredibly precious. Frog carried his father out into the garden each day to sit in a chair and feel the sunshine on his face and to take in the beauty of the plants he had tended over the previous 20 years. They shared his last meal together, laughing and remembering the many moments of a father-son relationship, easy in each other's company, completely trusting and just knowing the other. When the final moment arrived a few days later, we sat with his body, waiting for the doctor to come. His arms had held Frog as a baby, and had also been the first arms after our own to hold our twins when they were born—and now he was gone.

In the previous 25 years, whenever Frog had returned home from university, or home for Christmas, or home with me, his new bride, or home with his children, we would always say goodbye on the front step of the house, and his father would wave us off. He would carry on waving until the very last moment when the car went out of sight. On that last day the undertakers' car came to take him away ready for burial, and so Frog and I and his sisters stood on that step and waved. We kept waving with tears pouring down our faces until that car was out of sight.

I loved Colin. He was a dear and wonderful, loving, kind, funny and adventurous person. For my husband, he was Daddy. The person he still has the impulse to phone when he has a piece of news to tell or a funny story to share. The person whose reassurance he wishes he could seek for comfort or encouragement. The person he would like to receive advice from. The person who just knew things about him—because they shared so much of life together. But death means that this connection is gone. The loss never really feels totally settled or normal; it still surprises us at unexpected times—even years later.

THE COST OF LOVE

Suffering loss is the cost of having deeply loved. The New Testament includes a story about Jesus Christ as he stood at the tomb of his close friend Lazarus and mourned for him. The story contains the shortest verse in the Bible. John 11 v 35 simply says "Jesus wept". The next verse goes on "Then the Jews said 'See how he loved him!'" Jesus experienced what we go through when we lose a person, and it moved him to tears. The Bible includes stories like this which underline how powerful an experience of grief is and that this is not an experience that God absents himself from. Jesus himself went through grief; he himself experienced loss. His tears caused those watching to conclude that Jesus truly loved his friend— grief and love seem to be inextricably connected.

But perhaps we need to ask ourselves why does the death of a loved one hurt so much? And, on top of that, does what I believe about the world, God and life make sense of why loss hurts so much? Within the Christian story, losing a person hurts this much because a human is inexpressibly, eternally and undeniably precious. One Hebrew poet wrote:

> *For you created my innermost being;*
> *You knit me together in my mother's womb.*
> *I praise you because I am fearfully*
> *and wonderfully made.*   PSALM 139 v 13-14

43

Human beings are glorious, created, precious beings. We are not the product of random processes, indistinguishable in value from slime; we were "formed", and lovingly "made". Ecclesiastes speaks of the Bible's view that human life is not reducible by materialism and that, regardless of our beliefs or worldview, there is something eternal about us:

He has made everything beautiful in its time.
He has also set eternity in the human heart...

ECCLESIASTES 3 v 11

The book of Genesis describes how death, separation and sorrow came into the world as a result of human choices made initially in the Garden of Eden and subsequently reinforced by every human who has ever lived, as we considered in chapter 1. And so the cost of love—pain and suffering—impacts every person who has ever lived. However, a Christian understanding of pain through loss is not just informed by the beginning of the Bible. The middle and the end of the Bible also have something to say to us. In John's Gospel Jesus directly addresses the question of death—his own:

"Do not let your hearts be troubled. You believe in
God; believe also in me. My Father's house has many
rooms; if that were not so, would I have told you that
I am going there to prepare a place for you? And if I
go and prepare a place for you, I will come back and
take you to be with me that you also may be where
I am. You know the way to the place where I am
going."

JOHN 14 v 1-4

He speaks to his followers of the place where he is going as being a home that has "many rooms" but more than that he has gone ahead to "prepare a place" for them.

To those thinking about death, Jesus understands that we might be feeling disturbed or worried. He begins by offering his followers comfort "Do not let your hearts be troubled— trust in God, trust in me" and goes on to emphasise relational connection—"*I* am going there to prepare a place for *you*". But more than that, "I will come back and take you to be with me … where I am." Even the process of dying will be accompanied by Jesus, for any who will trust him. What extraordinary comfort for the loved ones of someone dying. Jesus will personally accompany them. The sting of separation is real, but a dying person who trusts in Jesus will never be alone.

I have read the words of John 14 by the bed of a dying person on a few occasions—including with a young woman dying of cancer and with a terminally ill baby and his mother. At these moments at the very end of a person's life I have noticed an electrifying sense of something more. It can be quite frightening to realise that the finality of death is almost upon us. But it was extraordinarily beautiful to think of Jesus being with my dying friend even at the very moment of death, taking her home and never leaving her alone even for a second.

THE END OF THE MATTER

The end of the Bible provides further insight into this question of where God is in our suffering and loss. As we have seen, Genesis tells us that the world was made "good" and things have gone wrong. We human beings have used our capacity to choose to bring darkness, sorrow, death, disease and loss into this world. But in Revelation, the last book of the Bible, God makes a promises about the end of time:

And I heard a loud voice from the throne saying,
"Look! God's dwelling-place is now among the people,

> *and he will dwell with them. They will be his people,*
> *and God himself will be with them and be their God.*
> *'He will wipe every tear from their eyes. There will be*
> *no more death' or mourning or crying or pain, for the*
> *old order of things has passed away."*
>
> REVELATION 21 v 3-4

That is an extraordinarily intimate image. Our crying eyes are so sensitive and tender. Many of us cry floods and floods of tears. As the mother of three boys I have often needed to mop up tears on the faces of my children. The promise in Revelation is that just as a loving parent looks into the face of their child and dabs their crying eyes as they comfort them, so God will wipe away our tears—and he will do that for all who turn to him. In these closing pages of the Bible there is an acknowledgment of the depth of the pain that people will experience in life, and an offer of eternal comfort and intimate connection with God. As I grieve for Brenda, that promise means a lot to me. It doesn't just make sense; it also sinks into my heart. It feels true.

NOT JUST A FEELING

However, central to Jesus' claims is that they don't just *seem* to make sense of our experiences and they don't merely *feel* true—they actually *are* true. The Jesus who wept at the tomb of his friend Lazarus was himself raised from death, validating his claims in a way that we can scrutinise by looking at the evidence. We can trust what Jesus Christ has to say about suffering, pain and death because he has revealed himself to be God walking in human history as a human being. And he has evidenced that claim by rising from the dead and leaving his tomb empty. He went through suffering and death and came back to life, and if this is true we have very good reason to listen to what he said.

So is it true? Did Jesus really rise from the dead? The earliest Christians were believers precisely because they had become convinced that Jesus had risen from the dead. At the earliest gatherings of the church, they habitually made a statement which the apostle Paul quotes. It's a statement that can traced back to Jerusalem in around AD 35, within five years of Jesus death:

> *Christ died for our sins, just as the Scriptures said.*
> *He was buried, and he was raised from the dead on*
> *the third day, just as the Scriptures said. He was seen*
> *by Peter and then by the Twelve.*
>
> 1 Corinthians 15 v 3-5 (NLT)

Summarising this evidence, both within the Bible and external to it, the scholar N.T. Wright concludes that...

> *... virtually all of the early Christians of whom we have*
> *any solid evidence affirmed that Jesus of Nazareth had*
> *been bodily raised from the dead. When they said "he*
> *was raised on the 3rd day" they meant this literally.*[9]

Proposing that Jesus rose from the dead was just as controversial 2,000 years ago as it is today. The discovery that dead people stay dead was not made recently; it was well known by ancient people.

The early Christians believed in the resurrection on the basis of overwhelming evidence—including Jesus' guarded tomb being found empty, and the resurrected Jesus appearing first to women at the tomb and then to his disciples on many occasions, including his appearing to over 500 people

---

9   N. T. Wright, *The Resurrection of the Son of God: Christian Origins and the Question of God,* Volume 3 (SPCK, 2017), p 34.

in one go. There are three facts of history agreed by almost all historians across a spectrum of personal belief systems about Jesus. These are:

- that Jesus died by crucifixion;
- that very soon afterwards, Jesus' disciples had experiences that they believed were appearances of the resurrected Jesus;
- and that just a few years later the Jewish scholar and persecutor of the church, Saul of Tarsus, also experienced what he thought was an appearance of the risen Jesus.

The vast majority of critical scholars also acknowledge as historical the empty tomb, the conversion of James (the sceptical brother of Jesus), Jesus' predictions of his violent imminent death, the earliest apostles believing that Jesus appeared in a bodily form, and the rapid growth of the early church.[10]

If we approach the evidence for the resurrection of Jesus without any prior dogmatic commitment to the impossibility of miracles, the only explanation that can sensibly explain the remarkable and agreed facts of history is that Jesus Christ really and truly did rise from the dead. There are many testimonials of former sceptical lawyers, philosophers, scientists, detectives and journalists[11] who became convinced of the validity of the resurrection of Jesus in the very process of investigating Christianity in order to disprove it.

---

10 For a very readable summary of this evidence from a professional historian, see John Dickson, *Is Jesus History?* (The Good Book Company, 2019).

11 For example, Simon Greenleaf, C.S. Lewis, Frank Morrison, John Warwick Montgomery, Alister McGrath, Lee Strobel and J. Warner Wallace have all written in detail about how and why they changed their minds about the resurrection.

The words of Jesus about suffering and pain don't just *feel* true—they *are* true. He has demonstrated that he can be trusted by rising from the dead. In the roller coaster of an experience of loss and grief, Jesus holds out the solid promise of a loving God offering us connection, closeness, comfort and presence. Where is God in suffering? He is right here—not in a fantasy world of religion or wish fulfilment, but existing and offering us relationship even as we experience the reality of our deepest suffering. The nature and scope of human loss is profoundly acknowledged in the Bible, which offers us a way of seeing the world that places sacred value on human life and connection.

In this way of looking at the world—through the Christian faith—our grief makes sense, and our sense of loss is validated and not glossed over. And in the midst of it all, we are offered connection, the presence of a loving God and hope for the future. The words of Jesus ring through the ages to us today when we experience the depths of grief:

> *Do not let your hearts be troubled. Trust in me...*
> *I have prepared a place for you...*
> *I will take you to come and be with me.*[12]

---

12 John 14 v 1-3

Sickness

*"Can a man who is warm understand
one who is freezing?"*
ALEKSANDR SOLZHENITSYN

In 2016 one of the most vibrant and dynamic human be-ings I have ever met, Nabeel Qureshi, was diagnosed with terminal stomach cancer. He was 34 and stood over 6 feet tall. He was a person of bustling energy. His stamina for teaching, travelling and engaging in conversation with the people who came to hear him speak was unmatched, and he did it all while studying for an Oxford University postgrad-uate degree—as well as being a father of a toddler.

Nabeel was the author of the New York Times best seller *Seeking Allah, Finding Jesus,* in which he tells the thrill-ing story of how he changed his mind about his birth reli-gion as he encountered Christ. He was someone who was continually intellectually curious and enormous fun to be around. When his friends and colleagues heard of his diag-nosis, it was impossible to take it in. How could someone so young, so fit, so vibrant, so *alive*—be dying? Nabeel had Stage Four stomach cancer: extremely difficult to treat and very aggressive. Three months before he died, I had lunch with him and we talked about all kinds of things. He was struggling with the physical pain of his illness, and the stabbing pain of the realisation that, bar an extraordinary miracle, he would not be around for his wife, Michelle, and their two-year-old daughter, Ayah, as she grew up. In this chapter we're going to consider the specific experience of suffering from a physical illness as we continue to ask, "Where is God in all the suffering?"

QUESTIONS

Why does nature go wrong? And where is God when illness strikes? Surely a loving God would not allow one of his most fervent and effective followers to die from cancer in his thirties, would he?

Sometimes serious illness can bring about real doubts in the hearts of the most fervent believers in God, let alone those who scarcely believe he exists. One powerful example of this can be found in the Bible in John chapter 11. One particular family who were very close friends of Jesus had this exact experience of faith being shaken. We saw in the last chapter that Jesus had a friend called Lazarus and that, when he died, Jesus wept at his tomb. But Lazarus had two sisters, and the family loved each other dearly. When Lazarus died of an illness, his sister Mary was upset that Jesus had not come soon enough to heal her brother. She said to him, "Lord if you had been here my brother would not have died." The illness and then death of a loved one caused Mary to doubt God. She is asking, *Where were you when this happened?* And she is alleging, *If you really loved us you would have been here and then this would not have happened.*

A similar thing may have happened to many of us. Someone is afflicted by an illness or premature death and we think, "God if you were here, or if you were real, this would not be happening". The fact that this very question is in the Bible and is directly posed to Jesus acknowledges what many of us experience. We struggle to reconcile the reality of cancer, chronic illness, impairment from an accident, the onset of a degenerative disease and many more experiences of illness and pain with the existence or presence of a God who loves us.

So if God is loving, why does our health go wrong? Why do we have to battle cancer, diabetes, coughs, colds, infections and so many other health niggles? How does the Christian faith attempt to reconcile its claims of a loving God with the painful illness and death of people, all the while claiming that God loves them?

THE STORY SO FAR

As we have seen, the Bible begins with a description of a loving and intelligent creator as the instigator and maker of a beautiful and good world. As Genesis unfolds, the writer describes how the possibility of loving relationships between human beings, and between human beings and God, requires a genuine decision-making capacity. True love cannot be forced. God created a beautiful, moral, ordered universe. Humanity decided to fracture that order by seeking not to love God, and instead to deny his authority over his creation and to live as rulers themselves. In Genesis 3 God makes very clear the consequences of that decision: death, thorns, thistles, disease, disagreement, heartbreak, pain. We live downstream from the decision of those first humans, in the broken world that their decision and God's response to it caused. We also contribute to that brokenness with our own decisions not to love others well, and not to love God at all.

Once human selfishness has a foot in the door in Genesis 3 the negative effects accelerate and increase through the rest of the book, until the direct connection is all but lost between a particular moral choice and the impacts of negative moral behaviour upon the very fabric of life. And so, whoever we are and whatever the particular decisions we may have made, whether they are good or bad, we will all be affected by this breakdown, and by disease and decay in our world.

According to the Bible our general human experience of disease is unaffected by our specific moral behaviour and even by our belief system. Whether we believe in God or not, every single one of us lives in a fallen world, and so we all experience the legacy of the choices made by other human beings reinforced over multiple generations as well as our own cycles of dysfunction and selfishness. The loving God who made a world in which love is possible did not choose to destroy us or discard us by hitting the reset button on creation. So does our continued existence in a world of pain and suffering show us that he is indifferent to our suffering? Not at all: the Bible repeatedly claims that God *does* care—that he does not ignore or abandon us.

At this point I think it is worth asking a "bigger picture" question. You see, whatever we believe about God, *all of us* are affected by disease and death—*but why do they hurt so much?* What does what I believe about the origins of life and whether or not there is a God have to say about why the suffering of disease and death matters so much to all of us?

WHY DO OUR BODIES MATTER?

When my children were born, I became friends with a woman whose son was born a few days before mine. The exhausting days and months with newborn babies and then looking after toddlers blur in a haze of memory, but my friend did it all while also coping with a chronic health condition of her own. The day-in, day-out grind of exhaustion was exacerbated for her by the constant pain she was in—but somehow she continued to care for her son. I don't know how she did it. And yet she is one of the most patient people I have ever met.

Two months ago I injured my back and was diagnosed with two herniated discs and a compressed nerve. I was housebound for five weeks, unable to drive and struggling to sleep due to the constant pain. I often thought of my friend, and realised just how much she had coped with and how little I had understood about what her life was really like. I began to realise that chronic illness, like other kinds of diagnoses, has a profound impact on us at the deepest level. Physical illnesses and wounds inflict something much deeper on a person and their loved ones than the brute fact of a raised temperature, immobility, bruises or cuts. There is a deep cumulative pain that seems to seep into the very core of who we are.

But why should the physical frailty of our bodies hurt us at this almost transcendent level? Could our human experience of illness be a reminder, an indicator, that to be human is to be more than a material entity of molecules and atoms? A Hebrew poet writing around 3,000 years ago put the sacred agony of illness into words that have given comfort to millions of people through the ages.

Hear my prayer, LORD;
 let my cry for help come to you.
Do not hide your face from me
 when I am in distress.

Turn your ear to me;
when I call, answer me quickly.
For my days vanish like smoke;
my bones burn like glowing embers.
My heart is blighted and withered like grass;
I forget to eat my food.
In my distress I groan aloud
and am reduced to skin and bones.
I am like a desert owl,
like an owl among the ruins …
My days are like the evening shadow;
I wither away like grass. PSALM 102 v 1-7, 11

Lament over illness is given voice in the Bible. Disease and death will hurt at the level of our most essential being if there is a connection between the real me—who I am—and my body. Suffering from an illness will have a deeper meaning than the physical experience of pain if our lives are created and sacred rather than random or purely material.

In my family this was brought home to me especially powerfully through seeing my stepmother-in-law experience breast cancer. For any woman, receiving a diagnosis of breast cancer is truly chilling. Given the widespread nature of this disease, most women will know someone who has died from it, and its location in such a significant place in the female body seems to evoke a specific kind of dread. Fleur was beautifully brave and resilient, funny and hospitable. And as the end drew near, her body was ravaged by cancer, but it was not so much the terrible pain of the illness that distressed her as much as the thought of the pain being inflicted on her daughters and husband whom she would have to leave behind. The acute pain of the loss and separation that was coming loomed larger, even as the physical pain intensified.

But there was also something sacred in that pain: the holding on to life—even as death crept up. It seemed to all of us that God was really present with us. On one evening we were together as a family in her bedroom, and we shared Holy Communion. This is a symbolic meal of bread and wine that Christians share to remember the crucifixion of Jesus, and the fact that he made this sacrifice for us. The bread represents Jesus' body and the wine his blood. Each of us ate and drank these physical symbols that look back to the cross, where Jesus suffered to make us whole, and look forward to eating with God's Son beyond the grave in a perfect, peace-filled world. We took these symbols into our physical bodies and were pointed to the hope of life beyond the grave.

Pain is real. Our human experiences of pain through illness, injury and physical suffering are truly devastating, but perhaps in being so significant, they also point us to the profound value and sacredness of life. Is it enough to categorise human pain as merely physical? Does it really make sense of our experience of illness and pain to say that we are nothing more than a collection of atoms? Is it enough to face death and "rage, rage at the dying of the light"?[13] or is there more to our human existence? Is there life in me beyond my body and potentially beyond the grave? Do illness and pain hurt this much because we are made in the image of God—made to LIVE? I think that we are created for life both *in* and *beyond* our physical bodies here and now, and Jesus uniquely makes sense of that. Where is God in our suffering of physical illness? If pain is the cost of love, our physical pain in illness is a consequence of living in this world where choices are made

---

13 Dylan Thomas, "Do Not Go Gentle Into That Good Night", *Poems of Dylan Thomas*, (J.M. Dent and Sons, 1973), p 159.

and love is possible. But in the darkest agony of physical pain, God has not left us to suffer alone.

WHERE IS GOD IN OUR EXPERIENCE OF ILLNESS?

This question has caused Christians to agonise and pray, to question and rage against God, but also, ultimately, to think about and care about palliative care. Since the very first days of the early church, Christians in every generation have been inspired to work with the destitute and dying. In the late 1990s I visited Mother Theresa's home for the dying. Mother Theresa was known for her work in Calcutta in India caring for the destitute, determined that every person be given a dignified death. The organisation she founded provided clean beds, food and drink, caring nurses and the opportunity for prayer for people who were terminally ill and living on the street. The home had simple caskets ready so that each person who came to them could have a decent burial. It was extremely moving to see the nuns, in their characteristic white and blue uniforms, lovingly tending to people whom others might consider untouchable.

In the UK, Dame Cicely Saunders is widely regarded as the founder of the modern hospice movement. Saunders' experience of caring for dying people and her belief that people could flourish even as they died were inspired by her Christian faith. Saunders and many of those who worked tirelessly for the subsequent expansion of hospice services were committed Christians, establishing hospices with the clear objectives of welcoming all who might need care and expressing the love of God through every detail of excellent provision for patients.

Where is God in our experience of pain? At least a part of the answer to that question within the Christian faith is that the Bible undergirds a commitment to the dignity of every human being, no matter how unproductive, unwell or incapacitated they may be. And so efforts to relieve the pain of others and create contexts where the whole person may flourish, including when ill or dying, are inspired by a commitment to God.

However, during an ongoing chronic illness and experience of pain, there can be a particular struggle around the question of healing when the potential of divine healing is held out. The inevitable question comes: if God exists, then why doesn't he consistently intervene on behalf of his followers in order to prevent or alleviate their suffering and show everyone else that he is real? Or at a more personal level: does God really love me? These questions are especially potent as God does *sometimes* seem to intervene miraculously and deliver people from danger, disease or death. But at other times heaven seems to remain stubbornly silent in response to our fervent prayers for healing and rescue.

DOES GOD HEAL TODAY?

Christians have wrestled with this dilemma—can God heal? If he can, then why wouldn't he always do it? If he doesn't heal, does that mean he doesn't really exist or does it mean he isn't really loving? There is a theological context to this question, which may help us understand the dilemma from the Bible's perspective, and grasp why Christians believe that even though God *does* heal some and not others, this does not mean that he is not loving or that he doesn't exist.

There appears to be a tension in the New Testament—with regard to God's miraculous actions in history—between what some people term "the now and not yet".

Jesus talked a lot about "the kingdom of God", or "the kingdom of heaven". It was the phrase he used to explain what he had come to do—to demonstrate the goodness, truth and reality of God on the earth. Those who place themselves under God's loving rule, will start to experience life as it was meant to be lived: Eden life—free from sin, suffering, oppression, poverty, pain and death. And Jesus demonstrated this truth by the miracles he performed: healing the sick, casting out oppressive spirits (demons) and even raising the dead. And there is strong evidence that this actually happened. One scholar comments:

One of the most compelling features of the whole sweep of ancient opinion regarding Jesus is his reputation as an exorcist and healer. It is no exaggeration to claim that it is one of the most widely attested and firmly established of the historical facts with which we have to deal.[14]

But Jesus spoke about the kingdom in ways that might seem strange. He said that "The kingdom of God is within you",[15] and yet that this means something very practical and physical: "the blind receive sight ... good news is proclaimed to the poor".[16] He spoke about the kingdom being present, and yet to come.[17] This future dimension to the kingdom, Jesus claimed, would come about when he returns at the end of time when there would be a final judgement and a new heaven and earth. This is when suffering will *finally* end. The kingdom, of which Jesus is the king, is both now and not yet: spiritual, and yet intensely practical.

---

14 James D. G. Dunn, *Jesus Remembered* (Eerdmans, 2003), p 670.

15 Luke 17 v 21 (World English Bible).

16 Luke 7 v 22.

17 And so the Lord's Prayer includes the future expectation "Your kingdom come" (Luke 11 v 2).

The miraculous interventions and healings that Jesus performed back then were signs that he was God's chosen king, who was bringing in the Kingdom.[18] In the same way, healings and miracles in the present are signs pointing us towards the certainty of this future reality of the kingdom which is both here now, but is also coming. A miracle is only a miracle if it is unusual. And in the Bible the usual laws of nature hold; miracles are seen and described as *unusual* interventions— signs pointing beyond themselves to help us realise something about who God is and what his kingdom is like. We can recognise a miracle and then its message precisely because it is out of the ordinary. Miracles are not deserved badges of God's special favouritism for the individual who is healed or helped, or rewards for good behaviour, but instead they are visible signs of grace and goodness, and tokens of hope by which everyone can see that this future judgment and the future bliss that Jesus spoke of are really going to happen.

Fourteen years ago I visited a member of our congregation who was in hospital dying of an aggressive cancer. He was a senior government official, doing tremendous, meaningful work for the protection of children nationally. He had a wonderful family and a strong Christian faith. We were devastated at his illness, and longed for God to heal him so this vital work could continue. But as my husband and I went in to pray for him he said to us, "A miracle is God's to give not ours to take." This humble, godly man was given a further two years of life against every medical prediction; he did have more work to do, but then he died peacefully with his family around him. It was a terrible loss—a brilliant man at the height of his career doing significant work in child protection, loved by his wife and his children. But to me he

---

18   The name "Christ" means "God's chosen King".

stands as a wonderful example of a Christian facing suffering, experiencing God's intervention and then his peace so he could face physical suffering and then death.

In my pain does God care about me? In contrast to other belief systems, Christian faith says *yes!* He *does* exist, and he *does* care. If we rule out the possibility of God existing, then all the universe has to offer us in our pain is indifference. In 1968, in an interview by Eric Nordern in *Playboy*, the film director Stanley Kubrick was asked: "If life is so purposeless, do you feel it's worth living?" Kubrick answered:

> *Yes, for those who manage somehow to cope with our mortality. The very meaninglessness of life forces a man to create his own meaning. The most terrifying fact about the universe is not that it is hostile but that it is indifferent… However vast the darkness, we must supply our own light.*[19]

In Eastern thought we would be at the whim of karma—that impersonal force which brings retribution upon those who deserve it through multiple generations of reincarnation. The fact of our suffering in some illness or another is a confirmation of our guilt, so you and I must simply bear the pain and just try to do better. The comfort that can be offered by meditation and fasting is offered in the hope of a better reincarnation in a subsequent life.

In other monotheistic faiths, God is transcendent, distant and only to be honoured and perhaps feared rather than loved or known personally. It is really only the Bible that tells us that we humans are precious and loved: that the hairs on our heads are numbered. And it is only Christ,

---

19 Gene Philips (ed.), *Stanley Kubrick Interviews* (University Press of Mississippi, 2001), p 73.

among many other "gods", who embraced the vulnerability of human flesh and experienced tiredness, thirst, pain and death so that God himself actually suffered. When we ask the question "Where is God in all our pain and suffering?", the Christian faith tells us that he is right beside us, knowing and loving us, and invites us into a relationship with him even as we suffer. This is genuinely unique. God himself has stepped into human history in Jesus Christ and suffered with us and for us.

This makes his love for us in our suffering knowable, tangible and real. The detective novelist and playwright Dorothy L. Sayers wrote:

> *For whatever reason God chose to make man as he is—limited and suffering and subject to sorrows and death—He had the honesty and the courage to take His own medicine. Whatever game He is playing with His creation, He has kept His own rules and played fair. He can exact nothing from man that He has not exacted from Himself. He has Himself gone through the whole of human experience, from the trivial irritations of family life and the cramping restrictions of hard work and lack of money to the worst horrors of pain and humiliation, defeat, despair and death. When He was a man, He played the man. He was born in poverty and died in disgrace and thought it well worthwhile.*[20]

In Jesus, God has experienced pain for our sake. He considered us worth that cost, and so in some sense our pain as human beings is dignified by his willingness to step into it.

---

20 Dorothy L. Sayers, "The Greatest Drama Ever Staged is the Official Creed of Christendom" in *The Sunday Times*, 3rd April 1938, p 1.

Mental Illness

"We need never be ashamed of our tears."
CHARLES DICKENS

My friend's 15-year-old daughter was having a full-blown panic attack. She was gasping for breath and thought she might be having a heart attack—her heart was racing, her chest was hurting and her hands were numb to the finger tips. Terror kept flooding her body in waves. All I could do was to talk calmly to her and ask her to try and take deep slow breaths: in for five seconds, out for five seconds.

The patterned carpet and fluorescent lighting of the conference room have been imprinted onto my mind—the fear was both palpable and physical. In her school this girl had numerous friends who were struggling with similar experiences of anxiety, or with anorexia or bulimia. Tragically she is not alone. Anxiety disorders among young people are on the increase. In the UK suicide is the biggest killer of men under the age of 35, and it is on the increase in many parts of the world.[21]

---

21   See en.wikipedia.org/wiki/Suicide (accessed 5th April 2020).

As we ask whether there is any meaning in pain, and consider whether God exists—and if he does, how that relates to our experiences of pain and suffering—this question of mental illness looms large for me. I feel that I am surrounded by mental illness as so many people I am close to suffer through it. There are young people who have attempted suicide in my community. I have friends needing to take time out from their jobs in order to recover from depressive episodes, all the while fearing that they may find themselves unable to support their families. The suffering caused by a mental-health condition is profound for the sufferers and for those who love and care for them. The anguish of the parents, siblings and friends left behind by someone who has taken their own life is indescribably awful. The suffering of loss is amplified by the sense that the person who died cannot have realised how their death would devastate those around them, and perhaps did not grasp how much they were loved.

The World Health Organisation reported in 2018 that "one in four people in the world will be affected by mental or neurological disorders at some point in their lives. Around 450 million people currently suffer from such conditions."[22] As the world has become more developed many more people have greater vocational and economic opportunities and greater access to resources than previous generations had. But it is surprising that this area of our mental health does not appear to have been helped by our economic advances. At the turn of the 21st century, several scholars began to argue that high material wealth can be associated with low psychological wellbeing. Consider

---

22 World Health Organisation press statement: who.int/whr/2001/media_centre/
press_release/en (accessed 8th December 2019).

the United States as an example. Psychologists observe that Americans now have far more luxuries than they had in the 1950s, but despite this, they are no more satisfied with their lives.[23] In fact affluence appears to be having the opposite effect.

The psychologist Oliver James points out that by far the most significant consequence of what he calls "Selfish capitalism" has been the startling increase in the incidence of mental illness in both children and adults since the 1970s.[24] Another psychologist D.G. Myers calls the conjunction of material prosperity and social unhappiness "the American paradox", noting that the more people seem to strive for money, the more numerous their problems and the less robust their wellbeing.[25] It seems that more affluent countries have experienced a significant increase in the incidence of mental-health disorders among their populations. Material wealth may not be able to provide us with substantial or comforting answers to this kind of suffering. In fact, pursuing materialism may actually increase our risk of unhappiness and mental distress.

But where is God in all of this? The suffering of mental-health disorders presents a very particular challenge to anyone considering the question of suffering alongside questions of faith since, if we are afflicted personally with a mental-health condition, our very perceptions, thoughts and feelings are affected directly. It follows that in this kind of suffering it can be peculiarly difficult to ask where God is, or to assert confidently that God is not there, since we

---

23 E. Diener, "Subjective Well-being: The Science of Happiness, and a Proposal for a National Index", in *American Psychologist*, 2000; 55:34–43.

24 Oliver James, *The Selfish Capitalist—Origins of Affluenza* (Vermillion, 2008).

25 D.G. Myers, *The American Paradox: Spiritual Hunger in an Age of Plenty* (Yale University Press, 2000), p 61.

may well start to doubt the trustworthiness of our own responses, reasoning and intuitions. Additionally, people of faith with mental-health disorders may have experienced condemnation from other religious believers for the very suffering that they are enduring. Suffering has often been compounded when people have been made to feel as if a struggle with anxiety or depression is an indication of weak faith in religious contexts.

Meanwhile, both materialistic atheism and rationalistic expressions of Christianity have tended to overemphasise the importance of right thinking in what it means to be fully human. For anyone who suffers with a mental-health condition, the pressure to self-correct through rational arguments—whether ideological or theological—may feel unbearable. It is difficult, if not impossible, to think yourself out of pain when the pain is felt in the very mind you think with. I think it is crucial to acknowledge the profound pain felt by the sufferers of mental-health disorders and those who are close to them. If you are going through something like that as you read this chapter, I want you to hear that your suffering really matters. It shouldn't be diminished as less important or less valid than other kinds of pain. It matters.

If it is true that an increasingly materialistic and less spiritual culture appears to be connected with growing mental-health challenges, is there anywhere we can turn? How might we begin to consider the question of where God is in the pain of mental illness? Different kinds of mental-health illnesses will be experienced quite differently, and so it might be helpful to consider what each worldview has to offer as well as the possibilities of the Christian faith.

DEPRESSION

Depression is a common mental-health problem that causes people to experience low mood, loss of interest or pleasure, feelings of guilt or low self-worth, disturbed sleep or appetite, low energy and poor concentration.[26] It is likely that many of us reading this book will either have suffered personally from depression or are close to someone who is suffering. You may even be in the middle of an episode right now or supporting someone. For many of us this will not be a theoretical issue.

What does depression really mean for who we are as human beings in an ultimate sense? If we do not believe in God or any spiritual realm, we may view humanity from a completely physical perspective, understanding every human experience at a purely physical level and focusing only on the material aspects of life. This philosophical viewpoint often leads either to a kind of utilitarianism—where human value, happiness and experience are measured by what we are able to usefully contribute or produce—or it can be expressed in some form of determinism—where a human life is entirely governed by our genetic makeup and the individual person has no real potential for choice, transformation or progress. From both of these materialist perspectives, depression is very debilitating, since any experience of it either vastly reduces human productivity and utility, or will feel like an utterly inescapable fate—the inevitable outcome of your genes.

Another way of looking at human experience if we don't believe in God is through the philosophy of dualism, in which the human mind, our thinking and rationality are paramount and the body is secondary. The body is thought

---

26 mentalhealth.org.uk/a-to-z/d/depression (accessed 8th December 2019).

to function as a kind of machine that is animated by the mind. However, if things start to go wrong with the mind— as happens with depression or any mental illness—it is experienced as an utterly fundamental problem that threatens to erase or shatter the very core of the sufferer's human identity. If *you* are essentially your mind *you* are in danger of being erased by a mental illness. This can be very frightening indeed.

From a Christian perspective, a human being is more than their mind and their body. A human being is created in the image of God as a mysterious union of body, mind and spirit—and the full sacredness of that reality is not destroyed when things go wrong. But perhaps more importantly, as human beings we are loved. God exists, and God is love. His love for us is not theoretical love; it is *actual* love. The Christian faith recognises the reality of depression— from a Christian perspective, depression is an affliction fracturing and dislocating our body, mind and soul. Like other kinds of illness and suffering it is a very real and painful consequence of living in this fallen world. But it cannot, and does not, define a person totally and therefore there is hope. You are unwaveringly, wholeheartedly loved—valued as precious, honoured as worthy of receiving eternal love.

If you are unfamiliar with the Bible, you may assume it is a book of unbending rules from a harsh and distant God who unrealistically demands perfection of us. Nothing could be further from the truth. The Bible is honest about our frailty as human beings and you don't have to look far to find people in it crying out to God from a place of mental anguish. Depression is experienced by people in the Bible, and those people are not shunned or shamed for it. They are embraced, understood and cared for.

A good example is the Old Testament prophet Elijah, whose story is told in 1 Kings 18 – 19. After Elijah experiences a huge victory against the prophets of Baal and the oppressive king, he runs away in fear. The text says that he…

> … *prayed that he might die. "I have had enough,*
> *Lord" he said. "Take my life; I am no better than my*
> *ancestors." Then he lay down under the bush and fell*
> *asleep.*   1 Kings 19 v 4-5

In the story, Elijah shows many of the classic symptoms of a depressive episode. And the question that Elijah and the writer of the narrative are asking is *where is God in this?* And the answer is clear: for Elijah, God was right there with him, encouraging him to eat and to live, caring for his physical needs, and eventually meeting him in a profound life-changing experience on a mountainside.

In the book of Job in the Old Testament, Job is a righteous man who endures horrendous suffering including severe depression. As the argument in the book unfolds, it becomes clear that depression is not presented as a consequence of individual wrongdoing, nor as a label of inadequacy for a human being. Depression is a terrible kind of suffering that many human beings will experience, but it does not have the capacity to diminish a person in any ultimate sense, even though it may make us feel sad, unproductive and hopeless. In the Christian faith, the experience of depression is placed in the context of the hope of the possibility of being restored. The believing sufferer can come through a depressive episode in this life, in the presence of a comforting God and in the context of a loving Christian community, all undergirded by the ultimate assurance that things will be restored completely and decisively in the life to come.

Where is God when depression hits? In the Bible he is close to those who are suffering; he offers an ultimate grounding for our worth and value, upholding our status as beloved and cherished people even though we experience darkness and depression as a result of living in this fallen world. We may well need medical support, medicine and talking therapies. We will certainly need the loving support of a community of people who are prepared to comfort, nurture and help us. But there is also a bigger picture: knowing that you are not alone and that this experience and this life are not the sum total of your existence. God offers us this hope in the context of relationship with him and in community with others that we were made to love and be loved. There is real comfort to be received from a loving God who does not deny the depth of our experience of depression but rather offers us an unshakeable foundation for our sense of identity and the value of our entire being—namely divine love.

SELF-HARM

Every time I have spoken to and answered questions from young people in the last year, some form of the question "Where is God in my self-harm?" has come up. Self-harm is when somebody intentionally damages or injures their body. It's usually a way of coping with or expressing overwhelming emotional distress. In *Self Harm: the Road to Recovery,* the authors explore theories as to why people self-harm. For many sufferers, their experience might be a combination of some of these factors:

- *Triggering endorphin release:* Endorphins are chemicals released in the brain that seem to help people relax and think clearly, as well as diminishing the impact of negative emotions and reducing pain. Physical injury triggers endorphin release, so people who self-harm are stimulating the release of these hormones to decrease their emotions and help them to relax.

• *Releasing emotions:* Overwhelming emotions that need to be processed might build up much like the air in an expanding balloon—and as the pressure builds, you can feel like you might burst! People who self-harm talk about how it helps them "release" those emotions so that they can get on with what they need to do in that moment or face another day.

• *Communication:* Another theory focuses on the way it can help people communicate or validate powerful emotions—to others or to themselves. A physical wound can be a kind of visible illustration of that emotional pain—much easier than putting it into words. While very few people consciously aim to harm in order to communicate (most self-harmers hide their wounds), the most common reason given for self-harm is that the sufferer yearns to have people hear their pain and to validate their distress.[27]

Self-harm thrives on the intrinsic connection between our psychology and our body as human beings, and it flies against dualism's assertion that the mind is everything and materialism's assertion that we are merely physical beings. Ancient cultures have sought to experience mental and spiritual release through cutting the body. The Old Testament describes the prophets of Baal doing just that in their showdown with Elijah. They called on their gods to answer their cries for vindication, and for fire on their sacrifice, and

---

27 Kate Middleton and Sara Garvie, *Self Harm the Road to Recovery* (Lion, 2008).

they intensified their experience by cutting their bodies. The writer notes:

> *So they shouted louder and slashed themselves with swords and spears as was their custom, until their blood flowed.* 1 KINGS 18 v 28

By contrast, the Bible affirms the value and preciousness of our bodies. In the New Testament, the bodies of Christians are described as being like the temple he lives in.

> *Don't you know that you yourselves are God's temple and that God's Spirit lives among you?* 1 CORINTHIANS 3 v 16-17

Our material bodies are not *all* we are but they *are* sacred and they do matter. Overwhelming emotions also matter— we have a Creator who acknowledges who we are and invites us into meaningful relationship with him, including the safe space to honestly communicate how we are feeling. Perhaps we can discern a disconnect between how we perceive things to be and how they actually are. We may think we are totally alone in the universe or that we are unloved or even unloveable, but are these perceptions actually connected to reality? If it is *actually* the case that a loving God exists, and that human beings made in his image are loved in an ultimate sense, then that would make a powerful difference. Grasping this truth—that we are loved—may help as an impetus to seek help and to recover from a pattern of self-harm. In fact, I have come to know many people for whom that is true. Years of cutting their arms and legs have led to many scars on the body, but experiencing the love of God has proved to be a turning point in stopping the cutting. One friend in particular shared with me how cutting had become a powerful release for her—it felt good. She felt that a cut had a kind of power to deal with her shame in a particular given moment and that because she deserved to bleed, the cut could help to shed her shame. She also felt powerful in that moment—no one was doing this to her; she was in control. When she truly experienced the love of God and meditated on Christ on the cross, she realised that Jesus' death for her, his blood shed for her was enough—she didn't need to shed her own blood anymore over her own shame or confusion or pain. And that helped her, alongside other therapies, to put an end to this self-destructive pattern that had got hold of her.

The Christian hope is an embodied hope. Christ walked this earth as "God with us" in a body. His death was real—his actual blood was shed. His resurrection from the dead shows us his authority over life and death. When we think about life after death, the Bible envisages an embodied experience of life that is different: "changed" from our current more difficult relationship with our bodies. 1 Corinthians 15 v 52 says: "the dead will be raised imperishable and we will be changed". A Christian can look forward with hope to a life beyond the grave without the affliction of alienation in our bodies—the Christian hope is embodied, and it is real, and that means that it can be a substantial support in the here and now when facing a struggle with self-harm. And it also helps us to understand why everything might not always feel completely right with our mind and our bodies.

SUICIDE

Are people who attempt suicide or die by suicide condemned by God? With the rise of nihilistic worldviews and social-media sites that encourage people to end their own lives, we might ask: where is God in the struggle and pain of suicidal thoughts? If this life is purely material and all that exists is physical why is it such a big deal to end a life? We may need to revisit the question as to why death by suicide hurts the friends and relatives left behind so profoundly if life is just a matter of physics and chemistry?

It is worth considering the role of faith in how we process suicide and specifically how a Christian might think about it. I believe that the reported rise in the numbers of people considering suicide in the developed world and the honest articulation of these despair-filled questions gives us an insight into the humanity of each person who asks them. Notice in contrast the power of the idea that our lives are sacred—that every human life is precious and imprinted with God's image. We human beings *are* made in the *image of God*. This complex and rich view of humanity chimes with the sense that human life ought to feel meaningful and fulfilling, as well as our sense of despair and dissonance when it does not.

If you are reading this and struggle with suicidal thoughts, I want you to know that I recognise the despair you feel. First and foremost, I would urge you to seek professional help as there may well be a chemical or medical cause underlying your suicidal impulses, or in the case of a traumatic or psychological underlying cause, therapy from a psychologist may be the most effective treatment. Just as you wouldn't say, "Just pray about it" or "Don't think about it" to a person with a broken leg, so with suicide the overriding advice should be to seek professional help.

At the same time, I would also want to point to the preciousness of your life, however you feel about it at the moment. This truth is not a blind, hopeful stab in the dark, rather, it has a coherent intellectual foundation in the Christian faith. The truth that there is hope and that your life is worth *everything*—to anyone who loves you and (whether you believe in him or not) to God—is a beautiful and powerful truth to cling hold of. John's Gospel says of Jesus that "in him was life, and that life was the light to all mankind."[28] Jesus is the source of life, and the intangible truth of the preciousness of that life is something that God can reveal to us in a very personal way. A deep revelation of the value of life is a legacy of genuine Christian faith.

The Bible does not only hold to an *imago dei* (image of God) view of human life in a kind of rose-tinted way, imagining that everything will be fine. It also recognises and describes the darkness of the world—including illness, death, depression and even suicide. These experiences are described and lived by characters in the Bible with real empathy and compassion. Sadly, mental illness was misunderstood for many years, leading churches to refuse Christian funerals or burials to those who died by suicide. But a careful reading of the Bible shows that it does not support that approach at all.

King Saul in the Old Testament ended his own life, following a military defeat by an enemy force and due to his fear after being wounded. Saul chose to end his own life, rather than face abuse by potential captors. When his attendant and armour-bearer refused the order to kill him, Saul took his own life by falling on his sword (1 Samuel 31 v 3-5). Saul's armour-bearer then, in total hopelessness at seeing that his king was dead, took his life as well. David's response was not to demand that Saul or his armour-bearer be vilified or shamed, but alongside his grief for his friend Jonathan, David mourned for Saul.

---

28   John 1 v 4.

> *And they mourned and wept and fasted till evening*
> *for Saul and his son Jonathan and for the army of*
> *the LORD and for the nation of Israel, because they had*
> *fallen by the sword.* 2 SAMUEL 1 v 12

A truly Christian response to suicide is to mourn, grieve and lament. Lament seems to hold together an acknowledgement of the agony with a refusal to deny the goodness of God.

Another Old Testament figure, Samson, in pursuit of revenge upon his enemies, used his final strength to push two pillars down which were holding up the structure in which he and a great crowd were standing. He took his own life along with the lives of many of his enemies (Judges 16 v 25-30). It was a tragic end to the life of a leader who had so much promise but was ultimately compromised and betrayed by his sexual liaison with Delilah. His death is not presented as deleting his identity or cancelling his connection to his family or to God. His family comes to collect his body and bury him with his ancestors. It is a deeply sad and poignant moment. Suicide is not an unforgiveable sin or an unmentionable embarrassment in the Bible as some have sometimes feared, but it is recognised as deeply, sacredly lamentable.

When we look at the Bible, I believe we never see suicide portrayed as the right choice, but always and primarily as a tragedy. The compulsion to end one's own life is far from how things were ever meant to be, yet for many people it is a real and terrible struggle. From a Christian perspective, life is sacred, and the fracturing and dislocation of body and soul are extremely painful, but even in the midst of experiencing these dark and overwhelming feelings, there is a genuine, accessible and robust hope for redemption. Every life is precious and filled with redemptive possibility whatever our own feelings of hopelessness might say. And so it would be wrong to determine the significance of a person's life by their productivity, utility to society, material, social or economic value. None of us are beyond the transforming hope offered in relationship with God. If you are struggling as you read this, or you know someone who is, please ask for help. Go to your doctor and ask for help. Seek the support of friends and family, and when you have done that, ask God to help you too. Your life matters; every life matters.

Mental-health suffering takes many different forms, and it is worth reflecting on how the way we see the world can account for the kind of suffering we may experience, and whether it offers any hope or help in the midst of the struggle. A further area of mental-health suffering that doctors have only recently begun to understand is the impact of trauma on a person.

TRAUMA AND ITS ONGOING EFFECT

Where is God in the aftermath of a human experience of trauma? Sigmund Freud described trauma as "an event of such emotional intensity that it breaks through the body's normal defences and floods it with an uncontrollable anxiety".[29] It is not only veterans of war who find themselves engulfed with post-traumatic stress disorder (PTSD). Survivors of abuse or a traumatic accident are likely to experience symptoms. In his book *The Body Keeps the Score,* Dutch psychiatrist Bessel van der Kolk describes and analyses how the human mind and body respond to trauma including substantial impact on our memories and a subsequent state of dissociation. This may be experienced as feelings of dislocation and total disconnection from people and events. Van

---

29 Sigmund Freud, *Trauma*

der Kolk writes: "Trauma is not just the event that took place sometime in the past; it is also the imprint left by that experience on mind, brain and body."[30] He continues:

> *The essence of trauma is that it is overwhelming, unbelievable, and unbearable. Each patient demands that we suspend our sense of what is normal and accept that we are dealing with a dual reality; the reality of a relatively secure and predictable present that lives side by side with a ruinous ever-present past.*[31]

In the world of psychological trauma, it is crucial to note the difference between conventional PTSD (which comes from a single trauma such as a car accident and can be treated fairly discretely and succinctly) and complex PTSD (which occurs as the result of repeated traumas on top of each other without time to process one before the next comes). This may occur in the form of consistent victimisation in child-hood, or torture during captivity in war, for example.

Improved therapies are now offered for treatment of PTSD and complex PTSD, but if our surrounding culture tells us that as a human being I am valued by my capacity to buy, to produce, to achieve and to think rationally, then when I am less effective, less productive and less rational due to having been traumatised, I am not just impaired as a person; my very value as a human being is under threat as is the point of my life, and that is deeply damaging. The Christian view of human beings as sacred image-bearers implies that a violation of that image is going to mean more than the brute fact of an event that you can get over quickly. Trauma will impact us deeply, but it cannot fundamentally

---

30 Bessel van der Kolk, *The Body Keeps the Score*, (Penguin, 2018), p 21.

31 *The Body Keeps the Score*, p 195.

diminish our personhood or damage our essential value. Nor can it separate us from God's love. In the Bible there is a promise for Christians that...

> *... neither death nor life, neither angels nor demons, neither the present nor the future, nor any powers, neither height nor depth, nor anything else in all creation, will be able to separate us from the love of God that is in Christ Jesus our Lord.*   ROMANS 8 v 28

My husband is a survivor of complex trauma as a result of the abuse he suffered as a child. As he has processed the complexity of recovery I have been amazed by the resilience and creativity of a person who has endured so much. I can see that alongside professional psychological support, love in a consistent, secure and safe relationship is crucial to recovery. Could it be possible that God is a heavenly Father who offers just such a relationship to every single one of us as the context for our healing? As we have seen, that is at the heart of the Christian message. As human beings we are loved—and the love of God is demonstrated, embodied and evidenced in history in Jesus Christ. Pain is the cost of love. We experience brokenness and pain in this world as a consequence of our freedom to make choices. The very same freedom that makes love possible also makes suffering possible. But pain is a cost of love that God himself is willing to bear with us and for us.

Is there hope when we are in pain mentally? Does this kind of pain matter—or are we better off embracing numbness and dissociation? Where is God in suffering when I have mental-health issues?

In the Bible God meets people in their pain. You are not required to get yourself well in order to experience the love of God for you or the peace of God that passes human understanding. Your pain is complex, distressing and meaningful—it really matters, yet it need not define or imprison you. God offers to meet you in Christ. He offers us the ultimate safety of a loving, eternal relationship. In fact the proof of his love for you and commitment to you is a man in a garden in deep mental anguish. Before Jesus' crucifixion, Luke's Gospel describes how Jesus was feeling as he was praying and preparing for his arrest: "Being in anguish, he prayed more earnestly, and his sweat was like drops of blood falling to the ground" (Luke 22 v 44). Hematohidrosis is a very rare condition of sweating blood when under enormous stress. Jesus Christ suffered tremendous mental agony as well as physical and spiritual suffering as he died on the cross for us. He is uniquely able to meet us in our mental pain and to offer a certain hope to us, rooted in his own suffering for us.

Dwell on that thought for a moment. Think about the possibility that you are precious to him—your breath, your body, your mind, your thoughts, your emotions. They matter to the creator of the universe. You have significance. The Christian story says that God entered the world in Christ because he loved you. Jesus told a story of a shepherd who had 100 sheep. When one of them got lost, this shepherd had such ridiculous priorities that he left the 99 to go after the one. Jesus told that story to illustrate how much God cares for the one, and that one is you, and it is me. This love of God is available to you and me whatever we might be feeling, and in full knowledge of all that we have experienced. Why not open your heart to him? As Jesus put it:

"Whoever comes to me I will never drive away."

JOHN 6 v 37

Violence

"If you are silent about your pain, they'll kill you and say you enjoyed it."
ZORA NEALE HURSTON

My childhood friend, who we will call Anna, told me one afternoon that she had been a victim of sexual abuse since she was eight. I could barely wrap my teenage mind around what that might even mean.

Anna's father came into her room at night three or four times a week and abused and raped her until, at 14, she disclosed what was happening to teachers and a youth worker, and with their help went to the police. There was a trial, and he went to prison. But Anna's mother struggled to cope and blamed her for the break-up of the family. As the teenage friends of Anna, our young minds tried to take this in— our beautifully courageous, wounded and heroic friend was being rejected *by her own mother* for exposing the horror of what had happened to her. This friend was 14 years old and felt that she had lost both her parents.

REAL-WORLD SUFFERING

It may be that as you read this book, an experience of suffering or pain feels pretty remote to you personally. Pain, for you, is more of an abstract "out there" thought rather than something you or a loved one has direct experience of. But for others, pain will be a searingly real and personal companion in life. It may be hard for you to philosophise or talk about it in the abstract because it is so close to home. As we consider in this chapter the question of pain as a result of the violence of others, I think it's worth trying to ground what we believe in realistic human experience.

Whether we believe in God or not, we all have a way of seeing the world, and within that, a perspective on suffering and pain. If our account of suffering or pain in the world has only been formed on the basis of relatively sanitised experiences of disappointment and cannot handle *actual* evil or extreme violence—then we need to ask ourselves whether it is truly adequate in the real world we inhabit? After all, a philosophy of life that can only work inside a bubble of niceness, untouched by the violence and evil that is so tragically common to the human experience, can't ultimately be rooted in truth.

I also want to acknowledge that there is a difference between experiencing apparently "random" suffering, awful as that is, and the pain of being hunted, exploited, attacked, raped, targeted or violated by another person, people or an army. And in an increasingly sexualised culture it may well also trouble us how easily a culture of disdain for another person can take hold in a group when fuelled to acts of violence by drunkenness and the desire for sexual gratification. The victim is casually discarded by those who think that nothing too bad has happened since she has no real worth, no importance, and she was drunk anyway. If a loving God existed, why wouldn't he intervene and stop an utterly evil thing being done to someone by someone? How can we hold a view that there is a good God when such terrible things do happen and he appears to do nothing about it?

We will all bring different experiences to bear on this question, and I want to acknowledge the horror that each and every one of those stories could evoke in us. But let me share a few examples of the type of suffering we are thinking about in this chapter.

My grandmother was an extraordinarily gifted and vibrant young woman. She was a brilliant musician and in other circumstances may well have become a concert pianist. But she was a woman in her thirties living in East Germany under Russian occupation and struggling just to survive. Virtually every woman in the community had been raped by a soldier. We rarely discussed what had happened, but I remember one day that she commented on how I rarely wore make-up and then went on to tell me that the women in her town would put flour on their faces and in their hair to make themselves look like old ladies in the hope that they would not be raped that day.

In my twenties and living in London, I made a friend who eventually confided in me that she was being terrorised at home. She felt silly and ashamed that she, an educated person with a job and friends, had somehow been caught in a web of domestic violence. Her partner—a charming, well-spoken man to the outside world—was an unpredictable tyrant at home who burned her with an iron when he thought she had disrespected him and showered her with praise, gifts and attention at other times. He belittled her and undermined her confidence in her own capacity to reason or remember things, and he had kicked her to the point of unconsciousness when his team had lost a football match and he had been drinking with friends. Her children were beginning to see what was happening, and she was living in a state of constant vigilance, trying to appease her partner and hoping that, if she could just keep everything as he liked it, she could prevent him from exploding.

A couple of years ago we received a call from an anti-human-trafficking organisation that we were supporting. A police raid had broken up a human-trafficking ring resulting in around 200 enslaved men being set free. They had been held as agricultural workers and kept in unspeakable conditions. While the prosecuting legal team prepared for trial, a vital witness needed shelter. There were potentially 200 witnesses, but it seems that all but one had been silenced with intimidation and threats to harm their family, or they had been murdered. This one surviving witness remained. *Could he stay with us to protect him in the run-up to the trial?* It was a privilege to help in this small way. He did testify in the end, and the traffickers were convicted. He had been violently abused by a gang of evil men, his compatriots had been brutalised and murdered, he had been traumatised and put through the ordeal of testifying, and his humanity had been challenged to the core.

Suffering can be inflicted by the evil of another person.

IS EVIL REAL?

One question I would like us to consider is this: does what you believe about good and evil, and the way the world really is, account for the depth of damage that one person can inflict on another? And just in case as you read this you think to yourself, "Well these are very extreme exceptional cases", let me tell you that the evidence suggests otherwise. For example, the increase in the number of women sexually abused in war since the Balkan conflict at the end of the twentieth century has led Inger Skjelsbæk, a research professor at the Peace Research Institute in Oslo (PRIO), to conclude:

> *We've gone from thinking that "rape is something that inevitably happens in war because men are men, and things happen" to thinking that rape is a clear war strategy and a war crime that threatens international peace and security.*[32]

Or we might look at the statistics of sexual abuse in the home in America: in 2017 there were 7.5 million reports of sexual abuse of children.[33] Or we could consider the plight of Yazidi women in the Islamic State era in Syria and Iraq. Or we could consider the abuse of children through grooming gangs in British cities. According to the UN's Trafficking in Persons Report, at any given time in 2016, an estimated 40.3 million people worldwide were in modern slavery, including 24.9 million in forced labour and 15.4 million people in forced marriage.[34] This equates to 5.4 victims of modern slavery for every 1,000 people in the world. These are a few examples among many that we could draw on as evidence of violence and sexual violence on a massive scale in our world.

As we ask the question "Where is God?" in the midst of

---

32 Kristine Grønhaug, "Rape as a weapon of war. Quiet, cheap and scarily effective." Norwegian Refugee Council Report, www.nrc.no/shorthand/stories/rape-as-a-weapon-of-war/index.html (accessed 4th April 2020).

33 *Child Maltreatment 2017*, Published January 2019. An office of the Administration for Children and Families, a division of U.S. Department of Health & Human Services. This report presents national data about child abuse and neglect known to child protective services agencies in the United States during federal fiscal year 2016. www.acf.hhs.gov/sites/default/files/cb/cm2017.pdf (accessed 4th April 2020).

34 *Trafficking in Persons Report, a Global Report of the United Nations*, 2018.

this horror, we should remember that in the Christian account of the world, the will of another person is explained and explored. Human volition, which makes love possible in this world, also makes evil a possibility. If we exercise our decision-making capacity for ill rather than for love, or prioritise love of ourselves or some other thing in the place of God, we end up with the world we see around us.

However, the biblical account does not leave us there. The Bible also tells us that God is our judge and that every person who has ever lived will be held to account for how they have lived:

> For he has set a day when he will judge the world with justice by the man he has appointed. He has given proof of this to everyone by raising him from the dead.
> ACTS 17 v 31

The Bible anticipates that many perpetrators of evil and violence will not be on the receiving end of human justice in their lifetime, but they *will* face the divine judge, and they will be judged for how they have lived:

> But they will have to give account to him who is ready to judge the living and the dead.   1 PETER 4 v 5

Christianity used to be criticised for being too judgemental—for threatening people with retribution in an afterlife in order to get them to moderate their behaviour today. But sometimes I wonder if we have lost sight of the goodness of judgment? Our hearts cry out for judgment if we care about the victims of evil. My love for my 14-year-old friend meant that when her father was convicted of sexual crimes against her, I felt relief and even thanked God that he was in prison. Judgment was good.

We might at this point also ask ourselves the question as to why evil hurts so much. If, as human beings, we are just a bunch of molecules and atoms, reducible to chemistry and biology, with nothing more to us than the matter of our physical existence, why does violence hurt so much? The brute fact of flesh being torn or bruised, the physical and biological truth of a sexual act, and the localised pain in the body of the victim, is a tiny dimension of the pain inflicted. Rape is an act of dominance, an attempt to dehumanise the person; it is an experience of evil. Violence meted out upon one person by another often feels like more than the sum of the physical acts carried out. At some level we all know this, but an acknowledgement of the depth of the evil of violating another person leads us to ask "Why?" As we have seen, key to the Christian answer here is that perpetrating violence against a fellow human being is to violate the image of God, and so there is a spiritual dimension to this kind of suffering.

In the Christian faith, God is the perfectly just judge. When evil things happen and we strive to see civil justice, we may not get the justice we hope for. But the promise of the Bible is that every single person will face judgement:

> *For we must all appear before the judgment seat of*
> *Christ, so that each of us may receive what is due*
> *us for the things done while in the body, whether good*
> *or bad.*   2 CORINTHIANS 5 v 10

Every rapist, every war criminal, every domestic bully. Every person.

The more we think about this, the less positive we might begin to feel about judgment, as we slowly realise that we might also be the perpetrator of evil against another person. The Bible seems to indicate that we are all both victims and perpetrators. Our oppressors will be held to account—and so will we. But for Christians, the good news is Jesus. Through his death on the cross, Jesus Christ has made a way for anyone to be forgiven; so that when we stand before God's judgment, Jesus has paid the penalty.

RECEIVING FORGIVENESS

Now it may well be that the degree to which we have hurt others seems microscopic next to rape or domestic violence. And so it seems even less like good news to hear that perpetrators can be forgiven because of the cross of Jesus. How can there be an equivalence between the "sins" of an ordinary person and the acts of violence of an abuser? The fact that a rapist's acts of violence and my propensity to shout when I'm upset equally need forgiveness makes the good news of Jesus seem obscene. But this is where we must take great care. God's offer of forgiveness through the cross of Christ is not saying that something bad happening doesn't matter any more, or that its significance is in some way *reduced*—on the contrary the thing *does* matter.

Christ's forgiveness acknowledges the absolute depravity and awfulness of the thing being forgiven, such that it demands that God himself had to die so that it could be paid for. And the magnitude of the cross of Jesus is that each and every failing, minor or severe, is individually borne by Christ. Receiving the divine forgiveness that he offers requires each of us to acknowledgment that we personally need it: to name our own failings and wrongdoing—and acknowledge how much we have hurt others.

In cases where that wrongdoing has involved law-breaking—including any case of rape, domestic abuse, child abuse or violence—it would also involve confessing to those crimes and being prepared to pay the civil penalty for them. The civil rights leader Dr Martin Luther King wrote: "True peace is not merely the absence of tension; it is the presence of justice." Christian repentance is not a private matter— and so the genuinely repentant person who can expect to receive forgiveness from Christ, cannot expect to avoid the civil penalty for a crime committed. An abuser who genuinely repents and becomes a Christian would willingly go to prison and pay the civil penalty for the crime they have committed if they have actually repented. Confessing and fully owning up to the wrong that has been done is our part in being able to receive forgiveness. For an abuser this acknowledgement must mean placing themselves into a context where they are prevented from harming others.

Christian forgiveness is not saying that a sin or a violation doesn't matter; it means saying that it really *does* matter. It matters because the very image of God in a fellow human being has been harmed, and this means that God, in Christ had to pay the penalty for that by dying an excruciating death, as he suffers separation from the Father taking the evil upon himself. God's forgiveness should never be glibly presented as a licence to get off scot-free in this life with impunity for crimes committed. It does, however, present the possibility of a relationship with God in the midst of this dark world if we will acknowledge the wrongdoing in our own lives and our need for help, for a Saviour. Christ offers the promise of his redemption through his suffering on the cross and a relationship that we can enjoy with him now and into eternity. When we are a victim of violence, the cross is very precious—he who endured violence and shame draws close to us. When we acknowledge the full horror of our own wrongdoing and its impact on our fellow human beings—whose lives and consciences are also sacred—the cross is unbelievably powerful. Dorothy L. Sayers wrote:

None of us feels the true love of God until we realise how wicked we are. But you can't teach people that— they have to learn by experience.[35]

In fact it is at precisely the moment when we acknowledge our own failings that we may be in a position to truly experience the love of God.

Sixteen years after Larry Nassar first sexually abused her, US Olympic gymnast Rachael Denhollander decided to publicly reveal that she had been one of the many victims of the USA gymnastics team doctor. She was 15 when Nassar started abusing her, and she was the first to publicly make allegations against him.

Nassar was found guilty of the crimes, and Rachel had the opportunity to speak to the judge directly before the sentencing. She pointed out that there are two main purposes of the criminal-justice system: the pursuit of justice and the protection of the innocent. On both bases she asked that Larry Nassar be given the maximum available sentences for his crimes. She asked the judge to focus on one question as she weighed up the decision, and the question was this: *How much is a little girl worth? How much is a young woman worth?* She urged that every person is worth every protection the law can offer, and that would mean they are worth the maximum sentence.

Rachel spoke directly to the convicted man and told him that he had used his daily choices to feed his selfish and perverted desires. She noted that the convicted man had

---

35 Barbara Reynolds (ed.), *The Letters of Dorothy L. Sayers: Volume Three 1944-1950: A Noble Daring* (Cambridge: The Dorothy L. Sayers Society, Carole Green Publishing, 1998), p 239.

brought a Bible into the courtroom and had spoken of praying for forgiveness. She went on to explain to Nassar that in the Bible God is so loving that he was willing to sacrifice everything to pay for the sin he did not commit. But she cautioned him that the forgiveness that he seemed to want from God could not come about by trying to do good—it would have to come from repentance. She explained that,

> ... *repentance requires facing and acknowledging the truth about what you have done in all of its utter depravity and horror without mitigation, without excuse, without acting as if good deeds can erase what you have seen in this courtroom today. The Bible you carry says it is better for a millstone to be thrown around your neck and you to be thrown into a lake than for you to make even one child stumble. And you have damaged hundreds.*

She went on to warn him that the Bible speaks of a final judgment in which God's wrath will be poured out on people like him. She pointed out that if he ever faced up to the enormity of what he had done, the guilt would be crushing, but that she hoped he could experience that and truly repent. She was prepared to extend forgiveness to him, but crucially this did not mean that she was asking for his crimes to be excused by the court. She said:

> *I ask that you hand down a sentence that tells us that what was done to us matters, that we are known, we are worth everything, worth the greatest protection the law can offer, the greatest measure of justice available.*[36]

---

36 youtube.com/watch?v=2nEvHeEUnVE (accessed 4th April 2020).

Larry Nassar received a 175-year sentence. On the basis of her Christian faith, Rachel offered him personal forgiveness *and* asked for the full sentence for his crimes. Justice matters if people matter. The question she asked the judge to bear in mind is so profound: *How much do we think people are really worth?*

Within the Christian faith people have infinite worth and value—every single person has been created in the image of God. And so it matters when something evil is done. Every wound inflicted hurts more than the brute physical fact of the act precisely because being human is deeply sacred. Where is God in this kind of suffering? His image is there in the sufferer, and he promises to hold to account in judgement every single person who has harmed that image in this world. But more than that, he himself was prepared to come into this world and be subjected to violent pain. Pain is the cost of love, as love enables the possibility of pain. But, for God, pain is a cost of love that he is willing to pay himself. In Christ, God himself has suffered violence and so if I suffer at the aggressive hands of others, I can turn for help and comfort to a God who is not remote or distant but one who is able to bear my sorrows with me. God was prepared to suffer with and for us, offering us the real and tangible possibility of hope, healing, forgiveness, justice and redemption in the midst of a dark and often violent world. He also stands as the ultimate Judge of all and, in the end, will bring perpetrators of violence to justice. That means that we can have confidence that God will call the violent to account and that those who appear to get away with their crimes in this life will need to face justice for them in the next.

Natural Disasters

"We can't prevent suffering.
This pain and that pain, yes, but not pain."
Ursula K Le Guin

In 2011, an earthquake in Japan killed 29,000 people. Just a few months earlier in 2010 an earthquake in Haiti left 230,000 people dead. In 2019 7.1 million people were suffering from starvation as a result of famine in southern Sudan. In fact, since 2016 more than 85,000 children have died in Yemen alone from starvation. In 2020, the COVID-19 virus took the world by surprise. The pandemic itself killed thousands, and millions have been harmed by the economic, social and other health consequences of the lockdown imposed by governments seeking to save lives. In all of this horrendous suffering, *where is God?*

The atheist philosopher David Hume summarises the problem as set out by the Greek philosopher Epicurus:

Is [God] willing to prevent evil, but not able? Then is he impotent. Is he able, but not willing? Then he is malevolent. Is he both able and willing? Whence then is evil? [37]

Hume considered this as a good starting point for rejecting Christianity. There are all of these horrible disasters around the world, he says, so God is either unwilling or unable to help. In either case he wouldn't be God. Therefore he must not exist.

It's a good point. If God is loving, why would he not intervene? Why would people be left to suffer and die in hurricanes, floods, famines and earthquakes? Surely natural events that kill hundreds and thousands of people are powerful and undeniable evidence that there is no God?

Every worldview must face up to the human suffering caused by natural disasters. Atheism might say, "This is how the earth is—there just *are* volcanoes and tsunamis and earthquakes and floods. That's reality—and so it doesn't matter in any moral sense. There is no moral framework within which this earth was created, and so it would be absurd to question the morality of a natural event that happens to kill people." The question lies firmly at the feet of Christians, who claim that there is a loving God behind the universe. Atheism has no case to answer here, and no reason to ask "Why?".

Others who follow a more Eastern philosophical influence might say that the universe is governed by the rule of karma, and so natural events like floods or earthquakes affect people in a cosmic cycle of reward and retribution. People who are caught up in seemingly random crises are actually paying for wrongs they have done in this life, or perhaps in some previous cycle of reincarnation.

---

37 David Hume, *Dialogues Concerning Natural Religion* (1779).

But what does the Christian have to say when faced with the devastating impact of natural events? Is Epicurus right? Do these events provide us with evidence that God is either not loving or not powerful—or non-existent?

Let's consider together a few points that might help us make sense of how there could be a loving God behind this world, in which people get caught up in suffering as a result of natural events.

The Bible makes the case for God being the creator of the universe and of this earth which we inhabit. And the earth that the Bible describes is the world as we know it—a world with mountains and volcanoes, oceans that rage and roar and rivers that flood their banks. Scientists tell us that our universe began as a result of the Big Bang, and that we live on ground beneath which there is a molten hot core upon which the tectonic plates of our continents float. That is how the earth works geologically. As an article in *Scientific American* pointed out:

> *Our planet is in constant flux. Tectonic plates ... jostle about in fits and starts that continuously reshape our planet—and possibly foster life.*
>
> *These plates ram into one another, building mountains. They slide apart, giving birth to new oceans ... They skim past one another, triggering earth-shattering quakes. And they slip under one another in a process called subduction, sliding deep into the planet's innards and producing volcanoes that spew gases into the atmosphere. And not only is Earth alive but it is a vessel for life. Because it is the only known planet to host both plate tectonics—that ongoing shuffling of tectonic plates—and life, many scientists think the two might be related. In fact, many researchers argued*

that shifting plates ... are a crucial ingredient for life.[38]

Earth is uniquely it seems, a "vessel for life" and this is in large part due to plate-tectonic movement. The same thing that causes volcanoes, earthquakes and tsunamis which kill people actually makes life possible at all. This is the way the planet works. We can think of many examples of good things that can also have catastrophic effects. The same law of gravity that enables my child to walk safely to school would also kill him were he to step off the roof of our house. Genesis 1 tells us that God made the world as it is and "saw that it was good". In order for life to have been possible on earth at all these natural events occur. The Bible describes the world that you and I experience including with its volcanic eruptions and earthquakes as God's "good" creation—a world in which plate tectonic movement appears to be crucial for life to have even been possible.

But it's not just about the origins of life. Plate tectonic movement is also essential for sustaining life on earth and regulating the temperature of the planet. Katherine Huntington, a geologist at the University of Washington explains:

Understanding plate tectonics is a major key to understanding our own planet and its habitability. How do you make a habitable planet, and then sustain life on it for billions of years? Plate tectonics is what modulates our atmosphere at the longest timescales. You need that to be able to keep water here, to keep it warm, to keep life chugging along.[39]

---

38 Shannon Hall, "Earth's Tectonic Activity May Be Crucial for Life—and Rare in Our Galaxy", *Scientific American*, 20 July 2017

39 Rebecca Boyle, "Why Earth's Cracked Crust May Be Essential for Life", *Quanta Magazine*, 7 June 2018.

In other words, in order for life to continue to be possible on earth, we need the plate-tectonic movement that causes natural events like volcanoes, tsunamis and earthquakes.

We see something similar with viruses. A pandemic such as COVID-19, SARS or Bird Flu might kill thousands of people, but each number represents a person: a precious human life. A dear friend of mine lost her mother to coronavirus in 2020. Due to the lockdown, she was not able to be at her mother's bedside as she died, and no more than two mourners were allowed to physically gather at her funeral because of the government restrictions in place to prevent the spread of the virus. How could a loving God allow viruses to exist that unleash such pain and trauma upon families?

Yet viruses are among the most abundant and diverse entities on the planet, and they are central to life. Marilyn Roossinck of Pennsylvania State University notes that...

viruses have traditionally been thought of as pathogens, but many confer a benefit to their hosts and some are essential for the host life cycle.[40]

She explains that less than one percent of viruses are harmful to their hosts.[41] John Lennox writes:

Granted that the science shows us that most viruses are beneficial and some are essential to life, why do there have to be pathogens that wreak havoc? The key question for theists is this: could God not have made a world without viral pathogens? This brings us to a

---

40   Roossinck, M, "The good viruses: viral mutualistic symbioses", *Nat Rev Microbiology* 9, p 99-108 (2011). https://doi.org/10.1038/nrmicro2491 (accessed 9th April 2020).

41   www.knowablemagazine.org/article/living-world/2018/why-viruses-deserve-better-reputation (accessed 9th April 2020).

whole class of similar questions. Couldn't God have made electricity that was not dangerous or fire that did not burn? [42]

If the vast majority of viruses are helpful rather than harmful to life, it changes how we look at the question of potential harm caused by the 1%.

Another aspect of this is to remember that natural events that can be experienced as disasters have also contributed to the extraordinary beauty of the earth. Mountains form when continental plates collide and shove rock skyward, where it can more readily be battered by rain. Weathering then slowly leaches nutrients from the mountains into the oceans. My grandfather was never happier than when taking in the beauty of the Engadine Mountains in the Swiss Alps. I remember gasping in awe when I saw them for the first time as a nine-year-old child from the window of a train. How could the snow be so blue and so white at the same time? I had not dreamed of such beauty existing. When I took my own three children to this same mountain range years later, I knew that their minds and imaginations would be forever expanded by the sight.

It seems that natural events like floods, tsunamis, virus proliferation and earthquakes are needed for life on this planet—they are only experienced as *disasters* because people die and are harmed by them. As we have already seen, the intrinsic sense of outrage and sorrow we feel when human beings are harmed—including those with whom we have no personal connection—is itself an indicator of the preciousness of human life, created in the image of God. Surely the best explanation for our reaction to the loss of human life in

---

42 John C. Lennox, *Where is God in a Coronavirus World?* (The Good Book Company, 2020), p 37.

the wake of a natural disaster is that life is precious and that it has a transcendent source.

THE FALL AND THE NATURAL WORLD

A further significant facet of this question for Christians is the story of Genesis chapter 3. As we have seen, the man and the woman, Adam and Eve, eat the fruit of the one tree they have been warned not to eat. As a result of their choice one of the things that is harmed is their harmony with the rest of the created order. This alienation between people and the natural world is poetically expressed by God as a curse—the consequence of moral decisions made by the man and the woman. Genesis puts it like this:

> *Cursed is the ground because of you; through painful toil you will eat food from it all the days of your life. It will produce thorns and thistles for you, and you will eat the plants of the field. By the sweat of your brow you will eat your food until you return to the ground, since from it you were taken; for dust you are and to dust you will return.*   GENESIS 3 v 18

Is it possible that the Bible is describing the impact of human selfishness upon the very fabric and environment of the earth? Human moral choices have led to a deterioration of the affiliation between humanity and the rest of the created order. Some theologians have extrapolated a connection between this "fall" of humanity and our alienation from the natural world to extend to a warning system that may help us survive natural events as some animals appear to have.

A huge tsunami rolled through the Indian Ocean on 26 December 2004, killing more than 150,000 people in a dozen countries. But, surprisingly, relatively few animals were reported dead. How did the animals sense the impending disaster? In 2005 *National Geographic* ran a piece entitled "Did Animals Sense Tsunami Was Coming?" The article pointed out:

> *Before giant waves slammed into Sri Lanka and India coastlines ten days ago, wild and domestic animals seemed to know what was about to happen and fled to safety ... Ravi Corea, president of the Sri Lanka Wildlife Conservation Society, which is based in Nutley, New Jersey, was in Sri Lanka when the massive waves struck ... Corea did not see any animal carcasses nor did the Yala National Park personnel know of any, other than two water buffaloes that had died, he said. Along India's Cuddalore coast, where thousands of people perished, the Indo-Asian News service reported that buffaloes, goats, and dogs were found unharmed.*[43]

Natural events are needed for the earth to be life permitting and life sustaining. They are not evil or wrong in and of themselves. The same kind of natural events that cause misery and distress are also responsible for creating outstanding natural beauty. Or is the problem perhaps that, as human beings, we have lost our innate ability to predict and so protect ourselves from these natural events through the fall described in Genesis?

But where does this speculation really leave us? In the face of any kind of suffering, it is completely understandable that we seek to attribute blame. And so, when children are killed in a natural event, we may wish to point the finger at God

---

43 Maryann Mott, "Did Animals Sense Tsunami Was Coming?" *National Geographic*, 4th January 2005.

and blame him. But the reality is that through experience, science and even Scripture we *do* know that as human beings we are living in a world in which we are vulnerable to natural events; they are a part of our planet. And as a human race we have intellectual and material resources to mitigate the effects of such events. But are we collectively and individually using those resources to help others? The reality is that the vast majority of people who suffer and die as a result of natural events are those who have been impacted by poverty, badly built buildings, poor governance, corruption, or by the environmental legacy of the selfishness of others. If we wish to accuse God of moral negligence, aren't we as human beings at least as guilty?

So, how do Christians see an earthquake or flood that kills thousands? Jewish culture during the time of Jesus had begun to hold to a tight cause-and-effect link between an individual's wrongdoing and disaster. They seemed to believe in a straightforward idea that "bad things will happen to bad people". But Jesus explicitly rejected this when he was asked about it:

> *Now there were some present at that time who told Jesus about the Galileans whose blood Pilate had mixed with their sacrifices. Jesus answered, "Do you think that these Galileans were worse sinners than all the other Galileans because they suffered this way? I tell you, no! But unless you repent, you too will all perish. Or those eighteen who died when the tower in Siloam fell on them—do you think they were more guilty than all the others living in Jerusalem? I tell you, no! But unless you repent, you too will all perish.*
>
> LUKE 13 v 1-5

Jesus was being questioned about a specific incident of unjust suffering that had just happened. He was asked whether people who had been murdered by Pilate had done something to deserve this. He widened his answer to include the random suffering of those who had died when a tower fell down and crushed them. And his answer in both cases was an emphatic *No!* Christians who follow Jesus do not see a natural disaster and conclude, "Wow—those people must have done something to deserve it!" Christians are *not* to judge those who suffer. But the suffering of people in such disasters *does* serve as a reminder to us that life is short and that this life is not all there is. Every single person who has ever lived will die and will face judgment. Earthquakes and other disasters are not themselves direct acts of judgment, but they are *reminders* of judgment. They can be read as warnings to us not to get too comfortable in this life, thinking we have everything together and no need of God.

But most of all, when a Christian sees an earthquake, pandemic or tsunami that kills or harms people, they should remember that the preciousness of each person caught up in that disaster is real. The sacredness of life rooted in the image of God underpins our response to disaster. We have good reason to feel outrage and sorrow, but also a real mandate to respond with compassion, generosity and self sacrifice. This is why, for all the failings of the church, wherever followers of Jesus have gone they have been known by their charity and philanthropy.

The ancient world did not look kindly upon the poor. Plato's attitude was typical:

> *The man who suffers hunger or the like is not the one who deserves pity, but he who, while possessing temperance or virtue of some sort ... gains in addition evil*

fortune. There shall be no beggar in our State; and if anyone attempts to beg, and to collect a livelihood by ceaseless prayers, the market-stewards shall expel him from the market, and the Board of city-stewards from the city, and in any other district they shall be driven across the border by the country-stewards, to the end that the land be wholly purged of such a creature.[44]

In the face of this pervading attitude, from the very earliest times, Christians were known for their charity. An early Christian book, *The Shepherd of Hermas,* repeatedly pointed to the Christian duty to take care of widows and orphans. Clement of Rome, another early Christian writer, praised hospitality and commended it in his letter to the Christians in Corinth as their main merit. He relates that many Christians went to prison voluntarily in order to set free others, and many of them became slaves so that the money paid for them could be used to ransom others. In his letter to Polycarp, Ignatius says that communities used their resources to ransom slaves.[45]

This is a trend that has continued to the present day. Studies in the United States show that church attendance is a key predictor of individual charitable giving in general,[46] and of giving to international causes more specifically. In Britain a report from the charity Cinnamon Network in 2016 estimated that two million people from faith groups who are mostly volunteers from churches, give over 384 million hours a year to projects like food banks, debt advice

---

44 Plato *Laws* 11.936 B-C trans. R. G. Bury, Vol II (Heinemann, 1926), p 465.

45 I. Zeipel, *Economic and Ethical Views of Fathers of the Church* (Moscow, 1913), p 249.

46 René Bekkers and Pamala Wiepking, "Who gives? A literature review of predictors of charitable giving part one: religion, education, age and socialisation", *Voluntary Sector Review* 2, no. 3 (2011): 337-365.

and family support. 288 million of those hours are unpaid. And so over 47 million people nationally are receiving support from religious groups every year. 2,000 faith groups around the UK were surveyed and, using the national living wage to value the time given by all groups, the study found that £3 billion or an equivalent of 0.4% of the UK government's total planned public spending of £743 billion for 2015/2016 was being donated for the public good by people of faith.[47]

In the words of Epicurus, we may well ask the question: *is God willing or able to help?* It is precisely into this arena that Jesus calls the church—to be his hands and feet in a broken and dying world. God in Christ did not remain at a distance, but he dealt with the evil in our broken world by suffering for us on the cross. And just as Christ died for the sake of others, believers are called to be willing to sacrifice, suffer and die. And the statistics seem to bear out that this is what is happening. While the church may fail at many things, the evidence suggests that, in this regard, Christians continue to follow in Jesus' way.

---

47 www.cinnamonnetwork.co.uk/wp-content/uploads/2019/10/26081-National-Report-CFAAR-20pp-2016-AW_hr.pdf (accesed 17th April 2020).

Systemic Suffering

> *"There are far too many silent sufferers. Not because*
> *they don't yearn to reach out, but because they've tried*
> *and found no one who cares."*
> RICHELLE E. GOODRICH

What does it feel like to be caught in a systemic cycle of suffering? In Peckham, south-east London, where I lived for seven years, many families have experienced five generations of unemployment, neglect, illiteracy and poverty. To be in pain because you are stuck in a faceless, impersonal system that grinds on and on is hard to imagine if you have not experienced it personally.

I remember taking a friend who had five children to the doctor's surgery to help her navigate the healthcare system for her youngest child. This vibrant woman had never learned to read. As we sat in the waiting room I had a sudden and powerful realisation that so many of the initiatives and systems designed to help her required her to be able to read the poster on the wall, the leaflet in her hand or the message on the screen in order to even begin to access any help. I caught a glimpse of how frightening and disorientating peoples' expectations of her must have felt.

Affluent people tend to get on with life and try not to think too hard about systemic suffering, particularly as the price of the phone in our pocket, the clothes on our back, the chocolate for our treats, and the fresh vegetables on our plates are affordable because of a global system where people far away live on low wages. The system works for me and my family, so it's not something I need to worry about particularly. But then from time to time the bubble is pierced, and news from outside the limited range of our own personal experience reaches us.

When Chinese workers in the main iPhone factory in China began killing themselves in large numbers in 2010, it became a story in the Western press. The corporation went so far as to install large nets outside many of the buildings to catch falling bodies. The company hired counsellors, and workers were made to sign pledges stating they would not attempt to kill themselves. The popularity of the iPhone continued to increase.

Even closer to home, the British nation was shocked in December 2018 to hear that a homeless man had died from cold outside Parliament, aged 43, while Members of Parliament debated legislation inside the chamber. The man, who was named as Gyula Remes, was found by British Transport Police outside Westminster Underground Station directly opposite the Houses of Parliament. A woman who knew him told the BBC, "He was blue last night, and everyone was just walking past him like he didn't matter". In the 21st century in an affluent, democratic, free nation a man lay dying outside Parliament because he was too poor to keep warm. He had found a job that was due to begin a couple of weeks later, but it was not soon enough to save his life.

In countries where corrupt and privileged elites hold down the vast majority of the population in poverty, human suffering is rife. Aleksandr Solzhenitsyn, who experienced Stalin's tyranny in the Soviet Union and was sent to the Gulag, wrote: "Unlimited power in the hands of limited people always leads to cruelty". The fact is that people can be caught up in a wider systemic injustice that is not a direct result of their choices or their body breaking down or a random accident or the particular pain of violence inflicted by one individual exercising their will on another. This systemic pain holds a peculiarly bitter kind of power because it dehumanises people on a massive scale.

Kalerwe is a large urban slum towards the north of Kampala—Uganda's largest city. Kalerwe sits on low ground that has historically been a floodplain. It does not have any sewage infrastructure so the latrines and gutters frequently flood and spread disease. Kalerwe is also home to Rachael, who I came to know when she arrived to study in Oxford on the course I teach. Through Rachael I have come to learn a lot about the situation for women in East Africa and particularly for women born into poverty.

I have discovered that girls are far less likely to be deemed worth the cost of an education than boys, and as a result many women become caught in a cycle of poverty. I have learned that girls are at very severe risk of early forced marriage, rape and prostitution from the age of eleven, and that giving them over to this kind of fate may give a short-term windfall to their families. I have learned that when girls start menstruating, they cannot go to school unless someone helps them manage their periods, and that beginning menstruation makes them an increased target for rape. I have learned that the plight of the girl child is humanly pretty hopeless without intervention from someone like Rachael. I have spent time in Kalerwe hearing firsthand the life experiences of many of these young girls and their struggle against a solid wall of systemic evil and hopelessness.

Where is God? Does God have any relevance in the face of great mountains of human degradation and pain such as we will find in Kalerwe and a thousand other slums throughout the world?

ANSWERS

The Bible explores the human experience of being caught up in systemic suffering. The Old Testament devotes an entire book—Exodus—to the experience of an enslaved people and their journey from slavery in Egypt to the challenges of being a nomadic people. The Old Testament prophet Jeremiah writes of his people exiled and oppressed by a foreign power. The generational oppression of invasion and foreign rule is expressed by the psalmist who laments "by the rivers of Babylon we sat down and wept" (Psalm 137). There is a whole book of the Bible devoted to an exploration of grief and lament for a people ravaged by war, violence and death—it is called Lamentations. The four Gospels were written about the life of Jesus Christ, himself born as a Jew into an occupied territory, the child of a refugee teenage mother. Jesus goes on to be unjustly accused and tried by a powerful and corrupt system of collaborators and Roman oppressors.

The pain of systemic injustice is not ignored or swept over by the Bible. It is a prominent concern in both Old and New Testaments, and a significant focus of the ministry of Jesus. When he began his teaching ministry, this is how he started:

He went to Nazareth, where he had been brought up, and on the Sabbath day he went into the synagogue, as was his custom. He stood up to read, and the scroll of the prophet Isaiah was handed to him. Unrolling it, he found the place where it is written:

> *"The Spirit of the Lord is on me,*
> *because he has anointed me*
> *to proclaim good news to the poor.*
> *He has sent me to proclaim*
> *freedom for the prisoners*
> *and recovery of sight for the blind,*
> *to set the oppressed free,*
> *to proclaim the year of the Lord's favour."*

Then he rolled up the scroll, gave it back to the attendant and sat down. The eyes of everyone in the synagogue were fastened on him. He began by saying to them, "Today this scripture is fulfilled in your hearing".   LUKE 4 v 16-21

Jesus' statement appears to be saying that he is God, and that he is focused upon bringing justice, mercy and goodness to the oppressed. And he seems to have expected his followers to do the same. In fact, the first Christians from the very earliest records were known for their practical love for each other, and towards people who did not share their faith when they were caught up in systemic injustice. In his letter James says, for example, "Religion that God our Father accepts as pure and faultless is this: to look after orphans and widows in their distress…" (James 1 v 27). The regular teaching of the early church is preserved in a document called the *Didache,* which could be translated "teachings" or "Homilies". It dates from the first century and it encapsulates the earliest and most vital teaching of the first Christian communities. The author urges Christians to "give to anyone that asks, without looking for any repayment, for it is the Father's pleasure that we should share his gracious bounty with all men".[48]

In the early second century, a church leader called Hermas argued in his influential work *Shepherd of Hermas* that the main requirement of the rich to demonstrate the genuineness of their Christian faith was to help the poor: "Assist widows, visit orphans and the poor, ransom God's servants, show hospitality, help oppressed debtors in their need".[49] In the second century, the Christian leader Ignatius of Antioch characterised heretics as those who "have no regard for love; no care for the widow, or the orphan, or the oppressed; of the bond, or of the free; of the hungry, or of the thirsty".[50] During a terrible epidemic that killed thousands in the third century, Dionysius wrote in an Easter letter around AD 260 that a substantial number of his church leaders, deacons, and laymen lost their lives while caring for others:

> *Most of our brother Christians showed unbounded love and loyalty, never sparing themselves and thinking only of one another. Heedless of danger, they took charge of the sick, attending to their every need and ministering to them in Christ, and with them departed this life serenely happy ... Many, in nursing and*

48 *Didache*, 1.1, 5. Quoted in William J. Walsh and John P. Langan, "Patristic Social Consciousness: The Church and the Poor," in *The Faith that Does Justice: Examining the Christian Sources for Social Change*, by John C. Haughey (ed.) (New York: Paulist Press, 1977), p 114.

49 *Shepherd of Hermas Mandates* 8:10 quoted in Walsh and Langan, p 115.

50 *Ad Smyrnaeans*, 6.2. quoted in Justo L. González, *Faith and Wealth: A History of Early Christian Ideas on the Origin, Significance, and Use of Money* (Harper and Row, 1990), p 101.

> *curing others, transferred their death to themselves and*
> *died in their stead ... the best of our brothers lost their*
> *lives in this manner; a number of presbyters, deacons,*
> *and laymen winning high commendation so that death*
> *in this form, the result of great piety and strong faith,*
> *seems in every way the equal of martyrdom.*[51]

Early Christian faith was indistinguishable from practical love for the poor and for those who were suffering. By the fourth century, Christianity had gained serious ground in the Roman Empire. But when the Emperor Constantine's nephew Julian wanted to take the empire back to its pagan roots, he found that Christian charity towards the poor was a significant obstacle. He wrote a letter to the pagan high-priest Arsacius saying that it was disgraceful that Jews and Galileans (Christians) never had to beg because they and anyone else in poverty were supported by Christian communities. He urged his fellow pagans to follow this example if they were to have any hope of resisting the growth of Christianity: "Teach those of the Hellenic faith to contribute to public service of this sort".[52]

In December 2018 an Indian newspaper ran an article reflecting upon how frequently religious leaders and gurus court the powerful and run after money, but how radically Jesus Christ challenges those norms. The headline in *The Wire* ran, "How Would Jesus Have Fared Amongst Contemporary Indian Godmen?" The author, Rohit Kumar, went on to explore how Jesus Christ or Yeshu Baba as he calls him, would have got on as an Indian holy man (Baba) today. He notes that

> *... patronage by the wealthy is essential for any Baba's*
> *career, which is why most successful Babas cultivate the*

---

51 Rodney Stark, *The Rise of Christianity*, (HarperSanFrancisco, 1997), p 82.

52 Quoted in Peter Brown, *Poverty and Leadership in the Later Roman Empire* (Brandels University Press, 2001), p 2.

rich assiduously. One should not hold it against them when they spend the majority of their time ministering to those with the means to fund their operations. It is good business sense to minister spiritually to those who can support you, and not waste too much time and energy on the poor masses.

Kumar had decided to read through the Gospels of Matthew, Mark, Luke and John in the New Testament to see how Jesus matched up. He concluded:

Had he been around, he would have most probably found no traction at all with the rich, the powerful and the religious. He might, on the other hand, have found huge appeal amongst the marginalised, the feminists and the liberal … Pro-service, anti-ritualism; pro-poor, anti-elitism; pro-women; anti-patriarchalism; pro-freedom, anti-orthodoxy; Yeshu Baba's career as a godman would have ended before it began.[53]

In a world enjoying a legacy of 2,000 years of Christian charity, it can be easy to forget just how significant Jesus' impact upon humanity has been as the instigator of a movement promoting the value of every human being, with an imperative to do something practical to respond to poverty and systemic suffering. John Gray, an atheist philosopher said,

One of the things I try to bring to the attention of secular humanists is that this aspect of modern liberal morality—don't be cruel to people—is hardly found in pre-Christian morality. It's a gift of Christianity and

---

of the theistic and Jewish inheritance that Christianity continued.[54]

Jesus' teaching has inspired Christians to work for the good of those suffering from systemic injustice. William Wilberforce, with his vision to see the abolition of the Atlantic slave trade in his lifetime, or the Earl of Shaftesbury, who worked for child labour and factory law reform, seeking better conditions for human beings caught up in the Industrial Revolution, are well-known examples of this impetus for social justice.

The truth is, of course, that Christians have also often been on wrong side of justice issues in the last 2,000 years. While Wilberforce campaigned for the abolition of the slave trade, Church of England bishops owned slaves, and many of the worst perpetrators of slavery called themselves Christians. While many of the earliest suffragettes in the UK drew inspiration from biblical imagery and were inspired by their faith, many in the institutional church sought to hold on to male dominance and resisted the impetus for votes for women. The institutional churches in America and Britain have not responded justly to the victims of child abuse who have called for justice when priests or clergy have abused them and have been ignored by bishops and elders.

We cannot skirt over this truth lightly: the church has done much that is good in social-justice terms, but there have been many instances of individual Christians and of the institutional church failing dismally to represent Christ and his ethic. For me, the key question when trying to make sense of such a confusing mixture of good and

---

54   www.newstatesman.com/2018/11/john-gray-rowan-williams-conversation-christianity-atheism-cambridge-literature-festival

evil is this: *what is the basis for those actions and positions?* When we read the Old Testament or look at the example and teaching of Jesus, the clear and logical conclusion is that the Christian worldview places a value on our neighbour and gives a practical imperative to care for the poor. And so the inspiration to start schools and hospitals, to fight for decent living conditions for children, or to care for the dying has been a driving force of Christian mission in spite of all the entanglements of colonialism and empire in the more recent developments in church history over the last 200 years. Jesus' ethic still calls his followers to demonstrate the love of God in practical ways in this pain-filled, systemically unjust world.

Where is God in the systemic suffering of people? He is present in his followers, who are working to overturn such systems in the very midst of the darkness of the world and to bring the love, light and truth of God's presence to all who will receive it. He is present in the intuition of sufferer and observer that this is not how things are meant to be. He was willing to be subjected to systemic injustice himself: to stand trial and be unjustly sentenced to death. A God who suffers and challenges systemic injustice is not remote or distant from this world. In fact there is a place that we can look at in more detail that brings God's involvement into clearer focus.

A place called Calvary.

The Suffering Servant

"Look at how a single candle can both defy
and define the darkness."
ANNE FRANK

"Surely he took up our pain and bore our suffering."
ISAIAH

W hy might history have looked forward to encountering a God who was prepared to suffer?

An Old Testament prophet called Isaiah beautifully foretold the coming into the world of a "servant of the Lord" who would willingly suffer pain and punishment for the transgressions of others. Isaiah spoke these words seven centuries before Jesus Christ was born:

Who has believed our message and to whom has the
arm of the LORD been revealed?
He grew up before him like a tender shoot, and
like a root out of dry ground. He had no beauty or
majesty to attract us to him, nothing in his appearance
that we should desire him. He was despised and
rejected by mankind, a man of suffering, and familiar
with pain. Like one from whom people hide their
faces he was despised, and we held him in low esteem.

ISAIAH 53 v 1-3

This "servant of the Lord" appears in a series of passages in Isaiah. Some understood this servant figure to be a Messiah—a longed for *anointed one*—who was to come in history and suffer for the people.

This suffering servant sounds so much like Jesus. He was born into the world as a Jew and grew up through the tenderness of childhood as an obscure figure going on to be despised and rejected by people and becoming familiar with the suffering and pain of the world at his crucifixion.

As Isaiah continues with his prophecy, he notes that the servant will be pierced, crushed, punished, have transgressions laid on him, and be oppressed and afflicted. It does not sound like a very happy mission in life. Isaiah writes:

Surely he took up our pain and bore our suffering, yet we considered him punished by God, stricken by him, and afflicted. But he was pierced for our transgressions, he was crushed for our iniquities; the punishment that brought us peace was on him, and by his wounds we are healed. We all, like sheep, have gone astray, each of us has turned to our own way; and the LORD has laid on him the iniquity of us all.

ISAIAH 53 v 4-6

Here, hundreds of years before Jesus died by Roman crucifixion, Isaiah prophesied that a special person would come in human history who would "bear the iniquity of us all." Who would carry our sins, our guilt, our shame, our darkness, our regrets. Who would be a god who suffers in our place.

This longing for a suffering god is in sharp contrast with the celebrated characteristics of Graeco-Roman deities. These ancient world gods and goddesses were figures who were to be placated, feared, obeyed and invoked. While there are gods and goddesses of the ancient world who die—such as Persephone, Dionysus and Osiris—there was no concept of an empathetic or self-sacrificing deity. A serving and suffering god is also alien to the teachings and preferences of the Buddha. Buddhism which presents suffering as *dukkha*—that which is ultimately to be avoided at all costs. As we have seen, for the Buddha himself that meant pursuing a life of detachment—since desire and attachment lead ultimately to *dukkha*. He lived what he believed—leaving home for ever on the night his son was born never to return to his wife or child for any contact. A suffering god who would suffer for us is in stark contrast to the ideals of Hinduism where suffering is a form of karmic retribution making sure that no bad deed even in a previous incarnation goes unnoticed. A suffering god is an anomaly in Islam which teaches that suffering is perceived as weakness—God would scarcely let a prophet suffer let alone be demeaned by suffering himself. But a suffering God is central to Christian faith and the cross of Jesus is at the heart of every expression and community of Jesus' followers.

A cartoon has been found on a wall in the ruins of ancient Rome showing how crazy the Christian message seemed to the people of that time. It's a caricature of Jesus' crucifixion, showing a man's body hanging on a cross—but the body has the head of a donkey (see next page). There's also a figure of a young man with hand raised as if in worship. Underneath is the inscription, "Alexamenos worships his god!" *A crucified god?* It was extraordinary; it was worthy of being mocked in graffiti by a satirist's scrawl. Greek and Roman deities were superior, distant, proud, far off; but never humble, self-sacrificing, and certainly never loving. A God who would enter our suffering world and die for us—be defiled for us, be shamed and suffer to pay a price for us—was earth-shatteringly funny to the culture of the first century.

Isaiah continues with his prophecy:

He was oppressed and afflicted, yet he did not open his mouth; he was led like a lamb to the slaughter, and as a sheep before its shearers is silent, so he did not open his mouth. By oppression and judgment he was taken away. Yet who of his generation protested? For he was cut off from the land of the living; for the transgression of my people he was punished. He was assigned a grave with the wicked, and with the rich in his death, though he had done no violence, nor was any deceit in his mouth. ISAIAH 53 v 7-9

Jesus was crucified between two thieves and then laid in the grave of a rich man named Joseph of Arimathea...

After he has suffered, he will see the light of life and be
satisfied; by his knowledge my righteous servant will
justify many, and he will bear their iniquities.

ISAIAH 53 v 11

The theology here is staggering. The violence of this death is shocking. Throughout the Old Testament there are prophecies of the Messiah—the anointed prince who would return and bring peace and justice. But here Isaiah predicts that the most appalling thing imaginable would happen; the Messiah, who was supposed to bring an end to violence and injustice, ushering in peace, was instead going to be the victim of murder. He would be "cut off from the land of living"— this language strongly indicates a violent death. He would be "pierced"—run through—suffering an excruciating and painful death.

Isaiah seems to be suggesting that the Messiah would bring an end to the brokenness of the world by being broken to bits himself.

The other-focused nature of his death is also shocking: the suffering servant was to be a guilt offering. In the Old Testament tabernacle and temple, an animal sacrifice could be offered which would take away a person's guilt—there was never, ever to be a human sacrifice. Yet Isaiah concludes this section by saying:

For he bore the sin of many, and made intercession for
the transgressors.   ISAIAH 53 v 12

The passage could not be clearer: that the servant being described would bear and carry the sins of the world *and* the punishment for the sins of the world. This death of the servant was *for* others—it would be what is sometimes called vicarious suffering.

The willingness of the death is also shocking. In the Bible, life is a sacred gift from God, which is why we cannot take our own life or the lives of others, since our lives don't really belong to us in an ultimate sense. But God's life is his own and, in Christ, he is going to lay it down for us in a staggering act of self-giving love for those who don't deserve it. Isaiah's readers must have been shocked and perplexed and amazed as they considered this. What kind of person *could* suffer for everyone else? Who could it be? The only answer to that question, unthinkable as it was, would that it would have to be God himself.

Jesus—as both fully God and fully human was able to truly be the man of sorrows—he can bear my sorrows and infirmities. Jesus—the one who is pierced when the Roman Centurion plunges a spear into his side—was run through for me. Jesus—the one who is crushed even as he dies the death of suffocation that crucifixion entailed—was afflicted and cut off for me.

The cross of Christ redefines *everything* because God in Christ has suffered pain voluntarily and purposefully for humanity. God in Christ did not brush over the issues and difficulties of human existence—he came into a world of darkness and suffering, and dealt with the reality of evil, suffering and selfishness by willingly experiencing crucifixion. Where is God in all our suffering and pain? God does not stay far off and observe our sickness and suffering from a distance. He himself has come. He has come to be with us and in his perfection to defeat evil. Karl Barth wrote that "God's own heart suffered on the cross". It was "no-one else but God's own son, and hence the eternal God himself". God suffers with us but ultimately God suffered at the cross for us.

Christianity is Christ. Coming to know him is akin to

discovering the answer to every riddle and to have thoughts flowing freely and clearly as if wind had caught the sails of our minds. Christ gives us absolute freedom from every cloying sense of guilt, sin and condemnation. Nothing comes close to the sense of release that floods a heart with the realisation of the total forgiveness of God. In one liberating moment, I came to see the cross as the saving act of God and know that he loves me even as he knows every corner of my soul and every thought in my mind.

The New Testament writers came to see that the suffering servant of Isaiah tells us that redemption has come ultimately through the suffering of Christ, but it also points us towards the redemptive possibility of suffering in the Christian life. The German Reformation leader Martin Luther called this a *theology of the cross*. Christians are shaped by Christ, and so our lives and experiences become cross-shaped. That means that we can trust that God speaks and shapes us in suffering. He does not cause the suffering, and he is not morally accountable for evil done that may end in our suffering, but in his sovereignty God can and does work for good in this fallen and dark world, even bringing about redemptive purposes in our suffering. Jesus' suffering was life-giving, and early Christians believed that their suffering mirrored that. Suffering was to be welcomed and embraced as an integral part of the Christian life. Another part of the Bible puts it like this:

And we know that in all things God works for the good to those who love him, who have been called according to his purpose.   Romans 8 v 28

The instinct to avoid suffering at all costs is not ultimately a Christian instinct. A maturing follower of Jesus will slowly but surely grow to not just accept suffering but to welcome it—as a part of following the suffering Saviour, as a way of knowing the suffering Lord more intimately, as an offering of worship to the suffering God, and as an act of witness in a suffering world. Suffering and receiving God's comfort enables us to be a blessing to other people.

> *Praise be to the God and Father of our Lord Jesus Christ, the Father of compassion and the God of all comfort, who comforts us in all our troubles so that we can comfort those in any trouble with the comfort we ourselves receive from God.*   2 CORINTHIANS 1 v 3-4

Suffering can even be a source of joy ultimately for a Christian because we know that it can make us stronger:

> *We also glory in our sufferings, because we know that suffering produces perseverance.*   ROMANS 5 v 3

Suffering may be welcomed by a Christian who draws closer to their suffering Lord, by experiencing his presence in the midst of disappointments, trials, illness and difficulty. Suffering might be embraced by a Christian who recognises that their capacity to endure hardship and grow in resilience expands even as they walk a difficult or challenging path. Suffering might be accepted by a Christian who realises that loss and love are so sacredly intermingled that love deepens and expands in the presence of sorrow. Suffering might be willingly endured by a Christian who is working towards the cause of God's love being known in the world and who knows that this cost is worth paying, even as it reflects the suffering of that loving God.

The "suffering servant" is the hinge point of history, and his followers do not seek to avoid being shaped by him—

not just by his words but by his cross. After all, it was he who said:

Whoever wants to be my disciple must deny themselves and take up their cross and follow me.

MATTHEW 16 v 24

Conclusion

"Someone I loved once gave me a box full of darkness.
It took me years to understand that this too,
was a gift."
Mary Oliver

We have journeyed together through the various facets of our human experience of pain and looked at how the God of the Christian faith interacts with our suffering. We have contrasted this view with other potential ways of looking at things, but we are still left with one rather obvious question. If all of this is true—if God exists and is ultimately known through Christ—*why did God go ahead and create us at all if he knew things would go this wrong and that so many would suffer such pain?*

Is God morally culpable for creating a world in which he knew people would suffer pain? Might it have been "better" for him not to have created at all? As I think about this question, I am reminded of my own dilemma as a young adult thinking about bringing children into the world. In my twenties I was living in a community surrounded by extreme examples of the pain of this world. My local church included members such as a mother whose son was murdered in a contract killing; survivors of the horrendous conflict in Liberia who had experienced extreme violence; children and young people caught up in the sexual violence of gang initiations; women who had experienced domestic violence and the grind of material poverty. Yet my husband and I went ahead and had our babies—twins first and then another. We did this knowing full well that our babies would grow and live in a world in which they will certainly suffer and eventually die. Love did not prevent us from having children—quite the opposite; love for each other and a belief that we would love our future children contributed to our decision to have a family. In the same way I think, we can conclude that love did not prevent God from creating us. Rather, love *inspired* creation.

From a more philosophical standpoint, we might point out the challenge of comparing existence with nonexistence and concluding that one would be "better". On what basis would we be able to make that value judgement, since we have no way of measuring "non existence". God's goodness is not undermined by his love, and his love undergirds our creation. The Bible tells us that the world as it is now is not as it was intended to be. Deep within our own psyches we might sense that we were created for something good and beautiful. In his book *Awakenings,* the great neurologist and author Oliver Sachs wrote about that intuition we have that all used to be well in our distant human past:

> *For all of us have a basic intuitive feeling that once we were whole and well; at ease, at peace, at home in the world; totally united with the grounds of our being; but that then we lost this primal, happy, innocent state and fell into our present sickness and suffering. We had something of infinite beauty and preciousness—and we*

lost it; we spend our lives searching for what we have
lost; and one day perhaps we will suddenly find it.
And this will be the miracle, the millennium! [55]

This instinct evokes the Genesis story. We were made for love, beauty and goodness in some primary way. But pain, darkness, selfishness and injustice have entered our world and are now a deep-seated if unwanted part of our felt human reality.

The outrage we humans experience in the face of injustice, death, disease or violence makes sense to us as human beings because we inherently sense that this is not the way things are meant to be. But is that really rational? Does our outrage make sense if we are merely material beings with no transcendent origin? Or is the very foundation of human outrage at evil and suffering a legacy of the image of God? Can a "survival of the fittest" worldview justify such outrage or does the Christian worldview have something really profound to offer us in the very fact that we raise this question of pain and suffering?

We have seen that genuine Christian faith is not about shutting down our human outrage at the violence or injustice of this world. Anger has a place in the Christian story, and every cry for justice and judgment echoes the essence of the Christian message. I hope you have also seriously considered that God can be found, known and experienced in the midst of pain through his own suffering.

Ultimately, at the heart of the Christian faith is the offer of relationship with a personal God who is not a system or a machine but a loving Father. A God who entered this suffering world in Jesus Christ, and suffered and died not only

---

55   Oliver Sachs, *Awakenings* (HarperPerennial, 1990), p 29.

with us but for us. Through his suffering, he can offer us redemption, forgiveness, safety and community. His comfort, strength and truth in our struggles and in our pain point us towards a hope-filled future; a home with him beyond the grave where we can be with him, comforted and loved enjoying eternity beyond the reach of pain.

He is only a prayer away from every single one of us. In the words of Jesus:

> *"Here I am! I stand at the door and knock. If anyone hears my voice and opens the door, I will come in and eat with that person, and they with me."*
>
> REVELATION 3 v 20

I wonder if you sense his voice speaking personally to you? Might you open the door of your life and invite him in? Why not pray a simple prayer to Jesus doing just that? Invite him into your life. Take a step towards inviting him into your pain.

Acknowledgements

No words could ever quite sum up how thankful I am to the people who have supported me and have been a part of this book. I would like to express my thanks to my husband, Frog, without whom it would not have been possible to write. Thank you for being a man who believes in sharing the load equally—not just excelling at what you do but being a true partner in life, at home and in the family. Thank you to my children Zac, JJ and Benji, for supporting me to work on this as well as in caring for you; your encouragement and honouring of creative and spiritual work mean the world to me.

Thank you to my very dear friend Nancy Gifford—not just for your inspirational leadership in this book series but for your unfailing love and for all the joy of our various adventures together. Heartfelt thanks to Sarah Davis, Ravi Zacharias and Sanj Kalra for the extraordinary love shown to me while I was writing this, and especially when my back was injured. Thank you to Mahlatse Mashua, Raymond Bukenya, Rachael Mutesi, Hassan John, Justice Okoronkwo, Paulson Tumutegyereize and Gideon Odoma. Your friendship and prayers have shown me how teams can become families.

Thank you to Tim and Vanessa Norman for the loan of your cottage for writing this, and to Tim Thornborough and everyone at The Good Book Company for all of your work on this project. Thank you to Dr Simon Wenham for your help with editing and to all of my RZIM colleagues around the world, and especially the Oxford team and the UK Board. Thank you to my colleagues and students at

OCCA—The Oxford Centre for Christian Apologetics—and particularly in this last academic year to Tom Price, Dr Max Baker-Hytch and Dr Sharon Dirckx. Thank you to Jasmine Wigglesworth for your incredible support of me as my executive assistant, but also for travelling with me this year; your friendship and encouragement have meant so much.

And finally thank you to my church family, Latimer Minster—a community in which love flows so poetically and practically and where I experience grace upon grace.

Can science explain everything? Many people think so. Science, and the technologies it has spawned, has delivered so much to the world: clean water; more food; better healthcare; longer life. And we live in a time of rapid scientific progress that holds enormous promise for many of the problems we face as humankind. So much so, in fact, that many see no need or use for religion and belief systems that offer us answers to the mysteries of our universe. Science has explained them, they assume. Religion is redundant.

Oxford Maths Professor and Christian believer John Lennox offers a fresh way of thinking about science and Christianity that dispels the common misconceptions about both. He reveals that not only are they *not* opposed, but they can and must work together to give us a fuller understanding of the universe and the meaning of our existence.

> *"This book is a remarkable achievement: engaging with all the big issues in just a few pages, while remaining profound, accessible, engaging and, to my mind, completely compelling."*
>
> Vaughan Roberts
> *Author; Speaker; Pastor*

thegoodbook.co.uk | thegoodbook.com
thegoodbook.com.au | thegoodbook.co.nz | thegoodbook.co.in

Why does God care who I sleep with?

SAM ALLBERRY

Few aspects of the Christian faith seem as jarring today as its teaching on sexuality. On any given day there are enough awful things happening in the world—injustice, poverty, suffering and environmental disasters. So why on earth would God concern himself with who we sleep with?

Best-selling author Sam Allberry has spent years thinking about, speaking on and discussing sex, sexuality and sexual identity with people from all kinds of backgrounds around the world. In this thoughtful and accessible book, he suggests that when we properly understand the teaching of Jesus on this most personal of subjects, we come closer to fulfilling our deepest longings than we might realise.

"Sam explores how the yearnings of our hearts, the instincts of our bodies and the complex cravings of our minds point us to something we want even more than sex."

Dr Rebecca McLaughlin, *Author; Speaker*

"Excellent answers to one of our generation's most pressing questions. If this is a question you've asked, wondered about or even just heard from others, this brief and thoughtful book will be a great help."

Andrew Wilson, *Author; Pastor*

thegoodbook.co.uk | thegoodbook.com
thegoodbook.com.au | thegoodbook.co.nz | thegoodbook.co.in

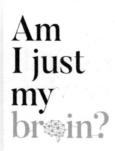

Am I just my brain?

SHARON DIRCKX

Modern research is uncovering more and more detail of what our brain is and how it works. We are living, thinking creatures who carry around with us an amazing organic supercomputer in our heads. But what is the relationship between our brains and our minds—and ultimately with our sense of identity as a person? Are we more than machines? Is free will an illusion? Do we have a soul?

Brain-imaging scientist Dr Sharon Dirckx lays out the current understanding of who we are from biologists, philosophers, theologians and psychologists, and points towards a bigger picture that suggests answers to the fundamental questions of our existence. Not just "What am I?" but "Who am I?"—and "Why am I?"

> *"Fresh, clear and helpful. Dirckx opens up a key part of what has been called the most important conversation of our time. Is freedom only a fiction? Is human dignity merely a form of 'speciesism'? Are we no more than our brains? The answers to such questions affect us all, and it is vital that we all explore them."*
>
> Os Guinness
> *Author; Speaker*

thegoodbook
COMPANY

thegoodbook.co.uk | thegoodbook.com
thegoodbook.com.au | thegoodbook.co.nz | thegoodbook.co.in

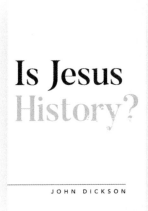

Is Jesus
History?

JOHN DICKSON

What can we really know for sure about the past? Can anything from ancient history be regarded as fact? In particular, how seriously can we take the historical sources for the life, death and resurrection of Jesus of Nazareth? Did he really even live in first-century Galilee and Judaea, or is he a figure of legend?

In this timely book, historian Dr John Dickson unpacks how the field of history works, giving readers the tools to evaluate for themselves what we can confidently say about figures like the Emperor Tiberius, Alexander the Great, Pontius Pilate and, of course, Jesus of Nazareth. He presents the conclusions of mainstream scholars—both Christian and not—and asks some pertinent contemporary questions, without offering any pushy answers. If Jesus really did exist, what are we to make of his own claims and those of his followers, and what would any of it mean for us today?

"An eminently readable and relevant introduction that debunks many misconceptions about the Gospel accounts of Jesus."

Dr David Wenham
Author; Tutor, Wycliffe Hall, Oxford

thegoodbook.co.uk | thegoodbook.com
thegoodbook.com.au | thegoodbook.co.nz | thegoodbook.co.in

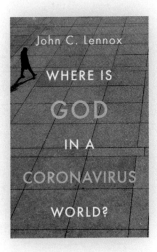

We are living through a unique, era-defining period. Many of our old certainties have gone, whatever our view of the world and whatever our beliefs. The coronavirus pandemic and its effects are perplexing and unsettling for all of us. How do we begin to think it through and cope with it?

In this short yet profound book, Oxford mathematics professor John Lennox examines the coronavirus in light of various belief systems and shows how the Christian worldview not only helps us to make sense of it, but also offers us a sure and certain hope to cling to.

"A clear, compassionate and critical read for these times. This book will give those who believe renewed confidence in why they believe; and it will help those yet to believe to find the key answers they seek."

Keith and Kristyn Getty
Musicians and songwriters

thegoodbook.co.uk | thegoodbook.com
thegoodbook.com.au | thegoodbook.co.nz | thegoodbook.co.in

the good book
COMPANY

Thanks for reading this book. We hope you enjoyed it, and found it helpful.

Most people want to find answers to the big questions of life: Who are we? Why are we here? How should we live? But for many valid reasons we are often unable to find the time or the right space to think positively and carefully about them.

Perhaps you have questions that you need an answer for. Perhaps you have met Christians who have seemed unsympathetic or incomprehensible. Or maybe you are someone who has grown up believing, but need help to make things a little clearer.

At The Good Book Company, we're passionate about producing materials that help people of all ages and stages understand the heart of the Christian message, which is found in the pages of the Bible.

Whoever you are, and wherever you are at when it comes to these big questions, we hope we can help. As a publisher we want to help you look at the good book that is the Bible because we're convinced that as we meet the person who stands at its centre—Jesus Christ—we find the clearest answers to our biggest questions.

Visit our website to discover the range of books, videos and other resources we produce, or visit our partner site www.christianityexplored.org for a clear explanation of who Jesus is and why he came.

Thanks again for reading,

Your friends at The Good Book Company

thegoodbook.com | thegoodbook.co.uk
thegoodbook.com.au | thegoodbook.co.nz
thegoodbook.co.in

WWW.CHRISTIANITYEXPLORED.ORG

Our partner site is a great place to explore the Christian faith, with powerful testimonies and answers to difficult questions.